CHATS ABOUT ELGAR

A PERSONAL VIEW
OF THE LIFE AND MUSIC
OF A GREAT COMPOSER

RICHARD WESTWOOD-BROOKES

To Mr Richard Nayar and his team at Hereford Hospital

Who made this book possible

By saving my life.

CONTENTS

INTRODUCTION 4
SO WHO WAS ELGAR? 6
MONEY, MONEY, MONEY 31
LAND OF HOPE AND GLORY 77
'ENIGMA' VARIATIONS 92
THE MYSTERY OF THE THIRTEENTH
                                        VARIATION 118
THE MYSTERY OF THE 'SOUL' OF THE
                              VIOLIN CONCERTO 136
THE DREAM OF GERONTIUS 166
WHEN ELGAR TOPPED THE BILL
                        AT THE MUSIC HALLS 182
THE MYSTERY OF ELGAR AND DELIUS 196

INTRODUCTION

For some years I have been giving regular talks about Elgar at The Firs, the little cottage where he was born, near Worcester, which is now a museum to his memory.

The idea of the talks was to provide insights into Elgar the man, his music and to certain aspects of his life with a view to introducing him to a much wider public.

While people in the music business, and 'Elgarians' as they like to call themselves know a great deal about him, recognising him as one of the great classical composers, many of the visitors to The Firs I speak to have little to no knowledge of the man and his music – other than perhaps a vague idea that he was a composer of such popular pieces as *'Land of Hope and Glory'* and *'Nimrod'*.

It has been a privilege to give the talks over the years, mainly because so many people come to me afterwards to say how much they had enjoyed what they heard and wished to listen to his music, so I thought it might be a good idea to put down in written form some of the thoughts I shared in the talks.

This is therefore a personal insight into who I think Elgar was, and to 'chat' about some aspects of his life and music. Those who know much about him may disagree with some of these thoughts and I accept that, but this little work is not really intended for those steeped in knowledge of the man.

It's offered as a few thoughts for those who perhaps don't know much about Elgar and his works, rather than some sort of in-depth musical analysis, or turgid reference volume, and as such it is intended as a 'good read' which will hopefully spark an interest in the reader to at least listen to some of Elgar's music – and perhaps even enjoy what they hear!

SO WHO WAS ELGAR ?

Many have pre-conceived notions about Elgar: that he was no more than a pillar of Edwardian Society, he only wrote music for state occasions, such as 'Land of Hope and Glory' and, with his military bearing, outrageous moustache and rather austere appearance, he was the very epitome of a British Colonial country squire.

Having lived with Elgar in my mind for more than 60 years, I have always felt that this has been a great injustice to the man. He was certainly much more than his image belied.

But first of all, perhaps a few biographical notes are in order.

Elgar was born in a humble country cottage at Lower Broadheath, a few miles from Worcester on June 2nd 1857.

His father was a piano tuner by trade, and shortly after Elgar was born, the family moved to their newly opened music shop in Worcester High Street where Elgar grew up.

Elgar's father had wanted his son to become a lawyer and the young Edward began training in a local firm of solicitors. But his bent was music and he left after a year, to earn a living as a performer and violin teacher.

Despite popularly held notions that he was penniless during this period, Elgar built up a decent enough living through his music, and also developed his skills as a composer – writing new music for the Worcester Glee Club, a gathering of all the best musicians in the area, and also for the County Lunatic Asylum Band where, at the age of just 21, he was appointed full time conductor and resident composer, producing music for regular concerts used as music therapy for the patients. He was also given opportunities to compose new music for a Birmingham based orchestra in which he played.

While this provided him with a growing reputation as a local musician, he nevertheless had dreams of being world famous – once saying that he would not feel satisfied until he received a letter from overseas addressed merely: 'Edward Elgar, England.'

His problem in achieving these dreams were, however, hampered by the fact that he had no formal musical education, and therefore no qualifications. He had hoped to attend the Leipzig Academy in Germany, then the most important musical institution in the world. But although the Elgar family were hardly destitute, they nevertheless had five growing children and could not afford to send one of them abroad for an expensive education.

So Elgar taught himself. He learned to play a wide range of instruments, and spent hours studying the music and tutors which were sold in the family shop – learning as he did the elements of composition, and forging the best of them into his own, unique, style.

This aspect of his development may have been remarkable, but it left an emotional scar from which he never fully recovered. This manifested itself throughout his life as an uncertainty as to his true value – a constant feeling of insecurity and inferiority, a wariness and resentment of academically trained composers, and at times a hatred of the whole business of music.

He was also a Roman Catholic at a time when the faith was only beginning to emerge as acceptable in English society, and many have suggested that attitudes to his religion amounted to discrimination throughout his life - though this is debateable. After all, most continental composers and performers were Roman Catholic and their faith never stood as a detriment to their success in this country.

If Elgar's career as a composer at this time amounted to no more than being a well-known musician in his local area then it was more to do with his own lack of drive and determination. It is all very well having dreams of great things, but in order to achieve them you must not only have the raw ability – which Elgar certainly had – but also the singular determination to succeed and put in the effort to achieve it. Settling for a reasonably comfortable provincial existence as a local performer and teacher was hardly the sort of springboard which would lead to greater things.

Everything was to change however when, in 1889, he married Alice Roberts, the daughter of a Major General from the Indian Army.

Coming from country gentry stock, Alice had a steely determination for her husband to succeed in his long-held ambitions. The idea of marrying someone considered 'below her station' in an era when class divisions were paramount brought stiff reaction from the two spinster aunts who had acted as Alice's guardians after her parents died, and she was warned that marriage to Elgar would inevitably lead to her being disinherited. This seems remarkable considering that she was, by this time, 40 years old, but Victorian conventions were strong, and their attitude left her very little room for manoeuvre.

It is most likely that they would have sounded out the general consensus concerning Mr Elgar's reputation, which may have concluded that it was not exactly perfect as far as his relationships with ladies was concerned and even that he was perhaps something of a 'gold digger'. In particular they may have spoken to the father of Gertrude Walker to whom Elgar is rumoured to have proposed marriage, and noted that he had stepped in pretty sharply to put an end to such things.

It might also be the case that the pressure they brought on Alice to abandon the idea of marriage was in the spirit of self-preservation. The arrival of Mr Elgar as the new head of the household would surely have threatened their sedate existence. They may have imagined their bags being packed the moment he arrived.

But Alice was determined to have her man and consequently abandoned the genteel lifestyle she had known to strive alongside him to achieve the fame for which he craved. She even converted to be a Catholic herself.

Being the daughter of a high ranking military figure, she was the sort of person for whom the word 'failure' did not seem to feature in her vocabulary, and within just seven years of their marriage, with her force behind him, Elgar rose from being merely a locally well-known musician to a position where he was hailed in the press as the *'greatest English composer since Henry Purcell in the 17th century.'*

For the next two decades, everything he produced seemed to turn to gold, and in modern parlance he might be considered to have achieved *'rock star'* status.

There were large scale choral works, such as *'The Dream of Gerontius',* brilliant orchestral pieces such as *'The Enigma Variations'* and *'Introduction and Allegro for Strings'*, two Symphonies, considered as great as any in the classical repertoire, two concertos, one for violin and one for 'Cello, and three fine chamber works – all of which were hailed by critics and public alike, and he became a truly internationally famous figure.

It came to an abrupt end, however, in 1920 when Alice died. He was said to been so devastated by the loss of his wife, that he virtually retired from composing altogether, only writing the occasional piece, but nothing of the great works of the previous years.

There was a very short revival towards the end of his life, when he started a fond relationship with a young musician named Vera Hockman, and he began writing another symphony and an opera. But time had run out for him and when he died in 1934 both works were left unfinished.

That, in a nutshell was Elgar's biography, but such a description is a chronical of what Elgar *did*. It is not an examination of who he *was,* which is a much more complicated matter.

As far as Elgar is concerned there are many opinions, based on varying assessment of his writings, behaviour and the testimony of those who encountered him throughout his life.

Interpretation of such evidence, however, has always seemed to me a personal matter, so I suppose it behoves me to provide my own opinion.

So who do *I* think Elgar was ?

After a lifetime of research and reading both the observations of others, and Elgar's own written word, I have long held the view that Elgar was as complex and disturbed a character, as any other great artistic genius you care to name.

But whereas others never shied from making public exhibition of the unconventional traits of their character – and are thus easily identified as 'cutting edge' 'alcoholic' 'drug induced' 'controversial' 'charismatic', 'avant-garde' and on occasions 'downright mad', Elgar successfully managed to keep the turmoil of his genius firmly within an outward display of Victorian and Edwardian propriety.

This would have been aided, if not promoted, by his wife, Alice, with her gentry background. When she married him – and given the rather harrowing circumstances and personal losses she sustained as a result - it is logical to assume that she would not have wished to have been regarded as the wife of a suburban music teacher – even though, that was, in effect, what she was.

Elgar thus became the sort of person she would otherwise have been expected to marry – dapper, well-dressed and groomed, remote, superior, only hob-knobbing with his class, and overall somewhat austere, and grumpy.

An aspect of what transformation Elgar underwent after his marriage can be seen from a printed card issued to autograph hunters which he produced shortly after he started to become famous. Its trite message reads: *'Dr Elgar only furnishes his signature on the express advice of his intimate friends.'* One is bound to wonder what many people in Worcestershire who remembered him as 'Ed' Elgar, the local musician, might have thought at receiving such a missive but the card had all the trappings of a pseudo-gentry status – ensuring that a suitable distance be maintained between them and the rest of us.

I guess he was willing to go along with this because it provided him with the emotional protection he needed – and it worked. Unfortunately, however, in terms of later assessment of who he *was*, perhaps this veneer was far *too* successful.

Because the real man underneath was much different from the confident, fashion-conscious 'Colonel Blimp' that he played. He was in reality an insecure, self-deprecating musical genius, always conscious of his 'tradesman's' upbringing and Catholic faith, and therefore awkward in company, particularly with those he might have regarded as intellectual or social superiors. A highly vulnerable passionate and emotional man who managed through his music to communicate such inner human feelings. It is no wonder that much of what he wrote was in effect autobiographical, and it is this feature of his music which has made it so appealing to so many people. Listening to a passage of one of Elgar's finest works, such as the ever popular 'Nimrod', you cannot escape the impression that you are hearing something written straight from the heart.

It is a tragedy that the *'real'* Elgar should have been so badly misunderstood by generations, but this is understandable, given that he so actively encouraged that misunderstanding by his manner, and so effectively buried the person who he *really was* under that *'pillar of the establishment'* image.

A great deal of what is written about Elgar came from people who knew him only in his later years – particularly during the 14 year period between his wife's death in 1920 and his own in 1934 – when he had withdrawn from active large-scale composition and was truly living the image of the country squire he had so painstakingly created for himself. Therefore we have scant evidence of what he was really like in his earlier days.

And this is made all the more frustrating by a tendency in published reminiscence to fall into the trap of what Sir Thomas Beecham, in his biography of his friend, the great composer Frederick Delius, referred to as a particularly 'British' trait – which is to try to make 'great' people into 'nice' people.

In the case of Delius, he observed, this was definitely not the case. But Beecham had sufficient status, being a genius himself, to be able to provide a forensically objective assessment of that particular 'great' man. In Elgar's case, there appears to have been no-one of similar standing who was prepared to commit his assessment to publication.

One who may have filled that role was George Bernard Shaw, the great playwright, who became a close friend in Elgar's later years, and would have provided a perspective from a similarly 'genius' level.

But he seemed to shun invitations to do so – only mentioning the occasional anecdote such as on one occasion he had advised Elgar to consult an osteopath during his final illness - which Elgar refused to do because it would mean he was consulting an *'unregistered practitioner'*. So, as Shaw put it : *'...he died, I believe, before his time, a martyr to the scrupulous conventionality he felt committed to.'* Shaw also, typically facetiously, said on another occasion that he could only comment on Elgar's *'somewhat bizarre personal habits'*.

I suppose another who might have provided informed comment was the great conductor Sir Adrian Boult who knew Elgar from a time when he was already established as a great composer, and who conducted his works throughout his career.

Michael Kennedy's 1987 biography of Boult discusses their relationship, mentioning that Boult from an early age didn't seem to have much appreciation of Elgar's music, and in particular his boyhood view of *'The Dream of Gerontius'* noted in his diary when aged 15 was *'I was very disappointed. It is a very aimless wandering...will Elgar live ? His 'Variations' will, I am certain. Will 'Gerontius' ? I am not certain by any means…parts of it are wildly exciting, but a lot is deadly dull…'*

And when I wrote to Boult many years ago in an attempt to elicit information, as I had believed at that time that this great conductor of many performances of Elgar's finest works would provide copious information about him, I had a surprisingly lukewarm reply: *'I have great sympathy with your passion for Edward Elgar but I am sorry to say I cannot help you. I occasionally met him and his wife but there is really nothing of importance that I can tell you about what he said or felt.'*

Furthermore many who *did* publish their memories of him were possibly in awe of his celebrity, so tended to provide a sanitised *'hero-worshipping'* chronicle of the man and his activities.

This view is borne out by one of the few who knew him in his earliest days – when he was a mere local musician in Worcestershire, plying his trade as a violin teacher. She was Rosa Burley, the Headmistress and owner of the private boarding school for girls in Malvern, where Elgar taught on a regular basis from 1891.

'To such an observer he was bound to present a picture very different from that seen by admirers who did not meet him till he was famous and who, deceived by the mask which in self-defence he had learned by then to adopt and by their own veneration for the musician, were often completely blind to the character of the man.

'Unfortunately the popular conception of Elgar's character today seems to be based very largely on the misconceptions of these admirers and we are almost asked to accept him as a lovable, if sometimes rather perverse country gentleman who somehow found time in the intervals between playing golf, getting himself knighted, taking long walks over the Malvern Hills, dining with Edward VII, sitting in various suitable London clubs and dressing like an elderly colonel, to become one of our greatest composers.'

For her own part, Burley chronicled her thoughts when she first encountered him in 1891:

'From various sources I had learned that he was not always good-tempered and that in consequence the girls were afraid of him.'

She then described her first meeting when she walked in on the music room at the school where Elgar had been playing the piano:

'A tall slight young man with a pale face and dark eyes rose hastily and rather awkwardly from the piano and stood scowling at me. Clearly the interruption was not welcome. Feeling rather chilled, I told him my name and said that I hoped his pupils were working satisfactorily. This elicited some sort of mumbled reply which struck me as, if anything, more hostile than his silence. He then stood blinking at me for what seemed a very long time until my struggle to think of some further contribution to this not very promising conversation was

mercifully interrupted by the arrival of [his] pupil. Somewhat deflated I withdrew.'

This first encounter was caused, through mistaken identity, with Elgar not realising that Burley actually owned the school. He had thought she was one of the chaperones who insisted on sitting in on his violin lessons with the girls.

But Burley does provide her overall impressions of the man she first met on that occasion:

'Superficially he was not attractive, his behaviour had been rather gauche and yet there was something about him that commanded attention. Here I felt was personality of an unusual kind.'

'The impression made on me at the outset was that he was extremely shy but that his shyness masked the kind of intense pride with which an unhappy man attempts to console himself for feelings of frustration and disappointment. I remember that as he entered the long room in which the lessons were given he assumed a simply tremendous dignity and spoke about all sorts of trifles but that when he came to the actual business of teaching he stammered, picked up ornaments, quickly replaced them and appeared almost unequal to the task in hand. He seemed to me to be a man whose emotional reactions were out of all proportion to the stimulating causes. It was thus very difficult to be at ease with him since he was so manifestly ill at ease with himself. At first I supposed that I might be the only person on whom

he produced this effect but I soon found that it was fairly general.

This remains one of the few published glimpses of the early Elgar, but it does reflect how he changed over the years, and when, in later life, he encountered someone as perceptive as the poet Siegfried Sassoon, we have perhaps one of the most complete pictures of the dichotomy of character which Elgar possessed.

Writing in his journals, Sassoon recalled encountering Elgar first hand in 1921 – about a year after his wife had died, when he was suffering all the grief and turmoil that ensued. Some might agree that he would naturally have been in a bad place.

By this time all Elgar's major musical achievements were behind him. He had written his 'Cello Concerto, the last great work he completed, two years before, and was falling out of favour with a new post-war generation who viewed him as someone from a long-abandoned Edwardian age.

So the Elgar that Sassoon met on that first encounter was a lonely man, disengaged from his past and trying to deal with the loss of his wife of 30 years.

'I go forth into the world alone as I did forty three years ago,' he wrote at this time, *'only I am disillusioned and old.'*

Sassoon was himself doubtless disillusioned and bitter - recovering from the abysmal treatment he had received from the British establishment for daring to speak out against the horrors of the First World War. So he was hardly likely to be kind in his assessment of a person who by that time had completely styled himself as the pillar of that very same establishment.

His first encounter was after a London concert which Elgar had conducted. Sassoon was in the company of Frank Schuster, the financier who had long been one of Elgar's friends and benefactors. The homosexual Schuster surrounded himself with young, attractive, male artists such as Sassoon, who he supported and promoted. Naturally, in this encounter, Sassoon took Schuster's side:

'Elgar was grumpy and unkind to Schuster (who has probably done more than anyone else to create his success) when he went behind to see him at the Queen's Hall – I was with FS (Elgar didn't notice me) & his behaviour made me quite bitter against him. He scarcely glanced at poor old Frankie who had come straight from Munich to the concert & missed his dinner to hear Elgar conduct; Elgar dashed out of the Hall & across to the Langham Hotel muttering 'You can come & see me at the hotel if you like'

There is no doubt that E is a very self-centred & inconsiderate man (how different to [Thomas] Hardy!).'

The following week Sassoon encountered him again, this time at Hereford, during the Three Choirs Festival, where Elgar conducted his great choral work *'The Apostles'*.

This meeting clearly bemused him, and underlined the dualistic nature of Elgar's character – the difference between the grumpy, off-hand 'country squire' he had met before, and the musical genius who lay beneath.

'Knowing how deeply he'd wounded old Frankie last week I made up my mind to be grumpy with E if I encountered him here !

'Selfish, conceited old brick' I thought. But, returning from this evening's concert early after hearing the concert I came into the hotel and there was Elgar, handing a letter in at the office window.

'And I could think only of the magnificence of 'The Apostles' this morning. Could this possibly be the man who composed that glorious work ? This smartly dressed 'military' looking grey haired man with the carefully trimmed moustache and curved nose ?

'And the great man actually seemed pleased to see me ! Was amiable & even modest in his manner.

'I wanted only to tell him of the delight I'd got from his music ! And of course I did so.

'He admitted that the final climax in 'The Apostles' had been 'pretty good' – I suppose he is very 'English' –

always pretending & disguising his feelings – anyhow that little encounter in the hotel entrance will always be a pleasant memory. I could almost wish that I might never speak to him again !'

But Sassoon did meet him again – this time in 1924 at Frank Schuster's beautiful Thames-side home at Bray, Berkshire, which in those days was known as 'The Hut'. It was here that Elgar spent many times during his composing career, and wrote large sections of his Violin Concerto and Second Symphony.

At this meeting, the 'country squire' was very much to the fore:

'Elgar arrived before tea. He looked rather puffy & old, & regaled us with his usual boring anecdotes about America etc. He greeted me affably, however, & said he'd like to go for a motor-tour with me ! asked what I am writing etc.'

There then followed a passage which he crossed out in 1950 when, perhaps he came to re-assess his more youthful feelings for the older man.

This is what he wrote in its un-redacted version:

'It is sad that I can't respect him. Long since I realised that he is a second rate man & I sometimes suspect that he is a second rate composer as well.'

That night, Sassoon and some of the other young house guests played a somewhat juvenile prank on Elgar –

which perhaps puts some of his comments into perspective:

'After Elgar went to bed we listened with suppressed giggles for the sound of the 'musical jerry' which had been placed in his room. Soon the tinkling little tune struck up to the intense delight of Anzie [one of the other guests] *who never tired of this urinatory witticism.'*

But the following day Sassoon encountered Elgar on his home ground – in the music room - a place, where he had composed some of the greatest music in the classical repertoire.

Here, Sassoon saw a completely different character:

'Elgar led me to the music room & played the piano for nearly an hour. It was delightful – He played snatches from piano music, Mozart A major Concerto, Bach Organ Fugue, Chaconne etc. After, I got him going on his own choral stuff - & he played through 'Death on the Hills', 'Te Deum', & 'Light of Life' making it sound superb. Quite sketchily unpianistic playing, but the rhythmic sense of course, wonderful –

'He also played some of Schubert's 'Rondo Brillante' (for piano & violin) long melodies – 'the best natural music ever written' he said (of Schubert as a whole). 'I could listen to it for ever'

'It was splendid to see him glowing with delight in the music – and made me forget (& makes me regret now) the 'other Elgar' who is just a type of 'club bore' at

lunch regaling us with long-winded anecdotes (about himself) he was a different man – the real Elgar was left in the music room.'

The following day the artist Walter Sickert arrived, and here Sassoon observed another trait in Elgar when he saw the two eminent men together.

After observing the following : *'At dinner EE wore sleeve links given him by Edward VII. W S couldn't possibly be imagined doing so ! Both like telling stories. E's are long-winded & trivial. S's tense & witty.'*

Sassoon then made the following remark, which, I think, sums up Elgar's innate defence of his own knowledge and intellect when faced with someone of similar artistic stature:

'W S knows nothing about music- which makes EE want to tell him about it. If S was knowledgeable about music EE wouldn't want to discuss it.'

This may have been a somewhat damning assessment of Elgar the human being, but Sassoon's reaction to his music matured over time, even though in those early days he might have considered Elgar a *'second rate composer'*. In later life, in a letter in my possession, he spoke of sensing Elgar's ghost in his library at his Wiltshire home, and remarked that he felt that Elgar was *'far my favourite modern composer – and he loved my poems also'*.

Correspondence exists between the two men, which perhaps also underlines Elgar's inner feelings of insecurity.

In one letter, from June 1923 Elgar remarked : *'I gather from the philharmonic that you most judiciously fled from the concert. I am sorry you don't like it...'*

And a few days later he wrote this: *'My dear Boy, how good of you to write: I am glad you feel the concerto but I am not thinskinned & love humour (and wit) & I could not help asking if you felt you had had enough in a good way or a bad way.'*

And in a further letter, dating from 1929 that insecurity once again came to the fore when he asked Sassoon whether he remembered him. Sassoon wrote a note in the margin *'Really, Sir Edward dear, you mustn't be so childish ! Not remember you indeed !'*

The exchange, it seems to me, is telling.

During his lifetime, and in the many decades which followed, Elgar has been regarded much more as that *'type of club bore'* that Sassoon observed – a pillar of the establishment. The writer of *'Land of Hope and Glory.'*

It is only in more recent times that people have begun to wonder whether this was truly what he was like. And the reason for that, lies in the music.

Just as Sassoon had observed, Elgar the musician was a completely different prospect to Elgar the 'country squire'. And when you listen to some of Elgar's finest pieces – the 'Enigma Variations', the Symphonies, the Concertos, the Overture 'In the South' the brilliant 'Introduction and Allegro for Strings' and the sublime slow movement of the Piano Quintet, it is impossible not to ask yourself the question – how on earth could 'Colonel Blimp' have written *that*?

This, of course, is where the true Elgar lies – in his music. This is where the more astute observer can discover what he was really trying to say, because this is how he made outward expression of his inner feeling – and that inner being was passionate, romantic, disturbed, emotional, in turmoil and sometimes perhaps even sinister. It is also, I think, what makes Elgar's music so particularly appealing to so many lovers of great music: it is *so* autobiographical, that you feel at times that you are in the presence of the man himself – pouring out his heart and the inner feelings which his constraints of conventionality prevented him from expressing in any other way.

It is also *the* paramount consideration. For without the *music* there is no reason to be interested in Elgar at all.

The dualistic nature of Elgar's character also derives from his background. Some observers have painted him as a person who could hold his own in sophisticated company.

But Elgar was a country boy. His famous saying *'I am still at heart the dreamy child who used to be found in the reeds by Severn side with a sheet of paper trying to fix the sounds and longing for something very great. I am still looking for this ...'* has often been interpreted as some sort of nostalgic looking back to the countryside of his roots by a man who had achieved the pinnacle of fame and sophistication. But it has always seemed to me that this should be taken much more literally – he *was* just a country boy who, deep down, was well aware of his limitations and awkward in company as a result.

Sassoon had observed this when Elgar met Sickert – eager to regale him about music in the knowledge that Sickert knew nothing of the subject – but if Sickert *had* possessed understanding of the art and was able to converse on the subject, Elgar would not have dared to speak to him about it – for fear of embarrassment at any perceived lack of knowledge.

In the same way, I have always been surprised that there is so little evidence in his letters that Elgar spent any amount of time discussing music with his peers. It is often observed that he remained wary of academically trained composers who followed him such as Vaughan Williams.

It is also, I think, worth mentioning that the underlying character that Elgar really *was* -i.e. the somewhat down-to-earth country boy – could emerge occasionally in places where you might least expect. In 1927, the year he reached 70 years old , for example, there were many ideas of commemorating the event through concerts of his music, celebrations in some of the best artistic venues of the land, and the undying hope that he might write new great music.

But instead of writing new music, Elgar was much more interested in making live recordings of his *'Dream of Gerontius'* – which would bring in far more money.

And as far as his entertainment was concerned that year, he admitted to a journalist that he, the greatest classical composer we had produced since Henry Purcell, had attended the London West End no less than 19 times to see a review entitled *'Clowns in Clover'* – featuring such songs as : *'Ladies **are** Running Wild, On the Wings of Love'*, *'Say No to Mr Gloom'*, *'Forty-Seven Ginger-Headed Sailors'* and *'There's a Trick in Pickin' a Chick-Chick-Chicken'*.

So when I come to assess who *I* think Elgar was, I have tried to imagine how *I* would have felt if I had been him.

He came from a tradesman's background. He was a Roman Catholic at a time when it was only just becoming generally accepted. He married into an upper tier of society at a time when class structure was paramount. He had no conventional education apart from basic schooling, and certainly had no academic training in music. He was the archetypal loner, living in his own world, gathering his knowledge his own way without the guiding hand of others who would have built into their instruction a questioning attitude - challenging whether this or that notion was fundamentally correct.

There was advantage in this. As many have observed, the mere fact that Elgar set himself on a course of self-instruction, adopting the best of what he read and rejecting the rest, ensured that the music he eventually produced was a hybrid that had not been pushed into any particular direction by academic training – and thus did not emerge as 'second rate Mendelssohn' or 'second rate Brahms', which has been the complaint of much of the music produced by other composers at the time.

Elgar's music did break new ground, fusing together the elements of the best he had learned but then further enhancing it with his own style – and it *did* lay the foundation for new beginnings in British music.

But there were disadvantages also to Elgar's approach, and these lay largely in his lack of understanding of the requirements of the business in which he found himself, and an awkwardness of behaviour in company – hence the observations of Sassoon and others that Elgar came across as *'grumpy' 'brusque in his attitude'* and somewhat remote.

And coupled with this was a life-long defensiveness in his character, which presented itself in outward expressions of often petulant behaviour which at times bordered on the juvenile.

But if I put myself into his shoes, so to speak, all this makes sense, and if I had been him, given the same social and artistic background and the constrictions of the era in which he lived, I would probably have behaved in the same way – and thus, having said that, Elgar comes over to me therefore as a real person, with all his faults and attributes, and a person that I can fully understand.

Trying to maintain an outward façade of conventionality when you are artistically frustrated within. Trying to hold your own in company in which you feel uncomfortable because you feel challenged by your upbringing in society, or your lack of artistic education. Suffering the frustrations that only a man of genius can endure – derived from a lack of fundamental understanding that what comes naturally to you is impossible to achieve by others. And having that Achilles-heal of arrogance of character which derives from knowing that you are superior to mere mortals in your abilities – but which sets you apart into a very lonely place as a result. These are the bedfellows of mental turmoil, and it is little wonder that many people of similar genius such as the composer Arnold Bax, who knew him, referred to him as having 'a troubled life'.

Having lived with Elgar in my head for more than 60 years – I can thoroughly believe that to be the case.

MONEY, MONEY, MONEY

One of the crucial features of Elgar's story which is often overlooked is the important role played throughout his life – by money.

In fact it's an aspect of all art which is largely ignored – yet money is fundamental to all artistic production – even, to some extent, controlling what is produced.

While the concept of the 'starving artist' dying for their art as they produce their maxim opus in a lowly garret, before being miraculously 'discovered' and put on the pathway towards fame, fortune, and eventual immortality might suit popular romantic fantasy – the reality is far from the truth.

'Artists' are, in biological terms at least, the same as every other human being on the planet, and as such have the same basic requirements for life. They must eat, drink, cloth themselves, put a roof over their heads, keep the winter storms at bay and do all the things that allow them, like the rest of us, to stay alive.

And that inevitably means that in varying degrees, they must pay life's bills – which means, equally inevitably, that they must in varying degrees also have access to money.

So if an artist, like Elgar, embarks on a career which relies, to a large degree in financial terms, on the success of his art, the commercial dimension, or in more basic terminology, the *money* he receives from his activities, artistic or otherwise, is one that plays a crucial role in his life.

This was not so much of a problem for some of Elgar's contemporaries, such as Charles Villiers Stanford and Hubert Parry, who both came from monied families, and also made successful careers in the academic world.

Elgar was not from such privileged stock. He was, after all, the son of a tradesman who might have made a decent living from his activities but was hardly wealthy enough to provide his son with a substantial private income which would allow him to devote his time to composition.

Lucrative rewards in the world of academia were also out of the question, as apart from basic schooling, Elgar had no educational qualifications. Despite his desire to go to Leipzig to train as a musician, his family simply could not afford to send him.

His father had attempted to provide him with a stable career by encouraging him to train as a lawyer – but he gave up in a year and from then on he had no option but to earn his corn from selling his artistic abilities as a musician.

For some years this provided a comfortable life, living at home above the family music shop in Worcester High Street, or lodging at his sister's home just down the road.

He could command a fee, in today's terms of about £250 per performance as a much sought-after violinist playing in local orchestras. From the age of 21 he supplemented these earnings with an income of around £3,000 per year in today's money, from his appointment as Band Master at the nearby Powick Lunatic Asylum. He also earned from conducting concerts as well as the fees he could charge as a violin teacher.

An indication of just how much he could command from his teaching is shown in one of client invoices. It amounted to the equivalent of about £300 for ten lessons. So assuming that each lesson would have lasted an hour, his rate would have been about £30 per hour in today's money.

But when, after his marriage in 1889, he embarked on the rocky road of becoming a full-time professional composer, the commercial realities of achieving the fame and moreover the *fortune* for which he craved, provided harsh instruction.

And that reality, to put it somewhat brutally, was this: 'art' is as much a 'commodity' as any other, assuming the 'artist' needs to rely financially on what they produce.

Just as with someone setting up a manufacturing facility to produce something like, say, screws, success in terms of financial reward cannot be achieved unless what you produce is what people want to 'buy'.

Equating great art to the production of screws might seem somewhat crudely simplistic, but the realities of market forces apply to both – if, that is, you wish to make a financially successful living out of either. Producing great art which appeals only to the artist, and a few select 'aficionados' but is otherwise unsaleable, might be spiritually satisfying to those few, but it will not pay the bills, feed the artist and his family, continue to sustain a roof over their heads, and keep them alive.

Similarly, if a screw manufacturer produces screws which don't sell, because they are either much more expensive than those produced by commercial rivals, or of the wrong specification, then the outcome will inevitably be the same.

I make this point because I think it is important to understand how the commercial world moulds and shapes the artistic one – and this was a vital feature in Elgar's story.

Anyone attempting to make a living from their art realises, if they are astute enough, that they must offer a 'product' which is saleable. And the corollary to that is that if they are *not* astute enough to realise this fact, then they will surely fail to make a decent living from their activities.

The artistic world is littered with those who have failed to make a commercial success – though, of course, this is not the sole benchmark for 'artistic' success. Far from it.

But the financial pressures of living and the often brutal requirements of those, such as publishers, concert and theatre promoters, and the likes of television and film producers who provide the vehicles which transform art into financial rewards, to say nothing of the reactions of the paying public who ultimately finance everything, often provides explanation as to why, for example, once great classical actors from a bye-gone age are seen years after their long past days of glory appearing in adverts for toothpaste. And indeed why so many of our otherwise 'mainstream' classical composers are known more for the incidental music they have written for TV shows and Hollywood block-busters than they are for the great opuses premiered to sparse audiences in classical concert halls.

There may be many, of course, who would consider this an over-simplistic and somewhat crude view of the world of art: that artistic achievement is the sole rationale and all other considerations are of little value.

This is certainly a laudable point of view – except for the nagging fact that I have yet to encounter any artist who has remained content in the knowledge that they gave away all their output for nothing in the spirit of artistic fulfilment , and then subsequently spent years witnessing others making vast amounts of money from the work they originally gave away.

So if you are an artist like Elgar, who *needed* to make a decent living from writing original music, then the commercial dimension unfortunately has a considerable bearing on your career.

As such, success in art can thus depend quite heavily, on what the commercial world 'demands', and the views of often hard-headed business people can have significant effects on what is actually produced.

In the case of Elgar this was certainly a paramount consideration. It is also the case that Elgar, in my humble submission, was, despite various views to the contrary by biographers and other commentators over the years, a hopeless businessman.

Had Elgar been sensible enough, or indeed, humble enough, to appoint someone to look after promoting his output, and deal with his business affairs, he might have been considerably more successful, in both money and artistic terms, than he actually was. Unfortunately, he didn't, and the scourge of money – or the lack of it – pervaded so much of his life.

Elgar's problem, as it seems to me, was that he lacked the sophistication required in his business dealings, and indeed displayed a naivety which at times was astonishing.

This was coupled with a tragic disregard for all matters to do with his business dealings – bordering on downright laziness - coupled with a belief that he could handle the business side of things without any input from anyone else.

This was displayed from the outset when he and his newly-wedded wife embarked on their adventure to establish him as a composer in London. Looking at the circumstances from today's viewpoint, it was bound to fail.

One of the first laws of success in business – if not in life itself - is that it's not so much *what* you know but *who* you know – and as far as Elgar's attempt to break into the London music scene was concerned, he knew hardly anyone.

When they arrived, he offered two new compositions to the publisher Novello & Co, because one of the few contacts he knew operating in the publishing world in London at that time worked for them.

This was the letter he wrote:

'Dear Mr Neale

With this I send two part-songs. I should be exceedingly grateful if you could bring them quickly under the notice of your firm. You may remember I have been requested to write for Worcester Festival & am very anxious to get some things introduced & published before that event. I heard this morning from Worcester & my people beg to be kindly remembered to you.

With many thanks and kind regards'

The recipient of this letter - 'Mr Neale' – was no executive of the firm, nor indeed anyone on the editing and publishing side of things. He was the sales representative who sold the firm's sheet music to the Elgar family business in Worcester.

Neale did in fact do well for Elgar, and Novellos accepted one of the part-songs – *'My Love Dwelt in a Northern Land'*, a setting of a poem by the Scottish poet Andrew Lang. However, they offered no money.

In exchange for the copyright, they agreed to produce 100 copies. There was no agreement on royalties from sales, and it is probable that the firm profited quite substantially from this arrangement as the part-song has remained one of Elgar's most popular to this day. Elgar, for his part, had 100 copies – and the requirement to distribute them himself at his own expense.

He nevertheless agreed to the arrangement, presumably under the misguided belief of 'jam tomorrow' and the warm satisfying feeling that his work was achieving publication by a leading firm. But this acceptance set the pattern for a relationship with the firm which would continue for almost the rest of his life. Elgar, the business people doubtless noted, was no hard-nosed negotiator.

Novellos had made their reputation through their dealings in the early part of the century with Mendelssohn, and firmly established themselves in the publishing world with the purchase of the copyright of his oratorio 'St Paul' – which was then followed by 'Elijah' – one of the greatest of all choral masterpieces.

They went on to have a lucrative business relationship with the leading composers both in the UK and abroad, including the likes of Gounod, Sullivan and Dvorak.

Having one of his works published by such an illustrious firm was no doubt gratifying to the unknown Elgar, but as far as Novellos were concerned, he was hardly any more important than the plethora of other composers at the time craving for success.

It is easy to view these early events with the hindsight of today and place them in the context of a scenario of a 'genius ignored'. This is, after all, a popular view about Elgar's early career. But these were business people that he was dealing with and they had a very clear-cut idea of their business model, and of course, had to continue to run a profitable business.

This is how the commercial realities of business can have such a significant effect on artistic output. Elgar might have had all sorts of ideas in his head of the type of music *he* might have wanted to write – but the reality was that if he offered such ideas to the likes of Novellos they would only consider what was within their business model, and what they might consider profitable. In the cut-throat world of Victorian commerce, they, like every other firm at the time, were no artistic charity.

The work which Elgar mentioned in his letter to Neale which he was writing for the Worcester Festival, the concert overture *'Froissart'*, naturally had to be considered within those parameters.

Elgar was understandably keen for them to take on his new composition – the largest work he had hitherto completed. The fact that it was to be performed in public at the Worcester Festival – one of the most important in the country – was certainly a boost to his fledgling career. But the idea of the work being taken on for widespread publication, was pure fancy.

The problem for this work, from Novellos' point of view, was that it was scored for a large orchestra. Publication would be expensive and, unlike part-songs and solo pieces which could be sold in their thousands throughout the country, the likes of a large-scale concert overture that could only be performed by competent forces – of which there were very few in those days - was an entirely different proposition from a business point of view.

So, despite the commission from the Worcester Festival, their reaction was lukewarm to say the least, writing that they might consider publishing it but adding: *'... there is so little demand for that class of music that we fear there is little probability of our undertaking it...'*

Eventually they agreed to 'publish' the overture, but what this meant was that in return for Elgar surrendering the copyright they agreed to print the string parts while the rest was hand copied and the full score manuscript would be retained in the firm's hire library as the conducting score. There was to be no money.

Elgar was apparently overjoyed that a work of his would be kept side by side in the library with the works of Mendelssohn, Dvorak, Gounod and Parry – but this was hardly financial recompense for his efforts in composing the work.

He was to receive similar lukewarm reactions to several compositions he offered at this time. But an indication of how the requirements of the commercial world shaped what Elgar *was* to write can be seen in the reaction he received when he offered Novellos the attractive *'Serenade for Strings'* – a piece which is one of his most popular today. This was their reply:

'We have given your 'Serenade' our attention & think it is very good.

'We find however that this class of music is practically unsaleable & we therefore regret to say that we do not see our way to make you an offer for it...'

Yet in the same year, Elgar offered them yet another part-song – *'Spanish Serenade'* – and this time they accepted it straight away – paying him the equivalent of £450.

The harsh realities of failure to establish himself in the capital as the commercially successful composer he had confidently believed he would be, finally led him to abandon London after two years and return to his Worcestershire roots, but it was also about this time that his most celebrated commercial failure took place, with the sale for just 2gns [about £165 in today's money] of his melody *'Salut d'Amour'* to the German publishers Schotts.

This went on to sell thousands of copies per month, and continued to do so throughout Elgar's life – being the melody of choice to accompany virtually every love scene in the music halls and the silent cinema, and played on barrel organs up and down the country. It is still extremely popular today.

Although Schotts paid him an additional 10 gns [about £800 today] in later years for various arrangements, Elgar never shied away from expressing the bitterness he felt at letting such a money-spinner go for such a pittance.

This is, of course, no unique phenomenon. Many artists rue the fact that they sold early work cheaply, only to see it gross rich rewards for others in later years. It was the same for Elgar's time as it is for rock bands and song writers today – who, with very few exceptions, have a similar tale to tell.

However, in the case of *'Salut d'Amour'* one cannot escape the fact that had he retained the copyright, it would undoubtedly have made him a millionaire. The song *'Roses of Picardy'*, a very popular song during the First World War, when it sold at the rate of 50,000 copies per month, made the equivalent in today's money of half a million pounds in royalties for its composer,

Haydn Wood while he was alive, and will continue to rake up royalties for his estate until 2029.

Another aspect of *'Salut d'Amour'* further illustrates how commercial considerations override artistic intention.

Elgar had originally called the piece *'Liebesgruss'* – a title with the same meaning, but in German. The publishers – though German themselves – felt that a French title for such a sentimental tune would make for a better sale, so it was published as such.

Elgar must have been furious, as his attitude towards French is summed up in a letter where he refers to that particular language as *'a vile and abominable tongue'*.

Yet, he had no control over the event – and this was repeated later on when he produced the attractive *'Chanson de Nuit'*. Once again, he wished for another title, suggesting *'Evensong'* or *'Vesper'*, but the publishers – this time Novellos – insisted on the French title, and so it has been ever since.

Commercial considerations came into play yet again when he received the commission from the North Staffordshire Musical Festival to compose his cantata *'Scenes from the Saga of King Olaf'* in 1896 – the work which really established him as a leading composer.

Elgar had wanted to write the piece in a free flowing, almost operatic style, but the publishers insisted that he write it along the same lines of Handel's *'Messiah'* – that is with the music broken up into a succession of self-contained elements, or *'numbers'*, as they are termed.

Their intention was clear. If the work was successful, then several of these individual elements could be published as stand-alone pieces and sold separately. So once again it was commercial considerations which overrode Elgar's artistic ambition.

Novellos were anyway somewhat reluctant about accepting it at all – initially requiring to see considerable portions of it before even considering publication.

They then required more substantive changes, resulting in this somewhat tetchy reply from Elgar :

'By this post I am sending the revised manuscript of King Olaf...now much curtailed: I have excised two recitatives & a solo besides many passages throughout the work.'

Money was once again hardly forthcoming. Elgar was to receive a Royalty of 3d [about £1 today] per vocal score but only after 500 had been sold – with a further Royalty of half that for separately published choruses. And in this regard they actually *did* publish a few of the *'numbers'* – and for some months forgot to let Elgar know, and equally forgot to pay him any royalties.

In addition, *he* had to guarantee financially the whole production out of his own pocket to the tune of about £5,000 in today's money. They were certainly ensuring that they would not suffer financially as a result of the production.

In the event, the work was a tremendous success at its first performance, and a second showing was arranged for the Crystal Palace in London. At last, Elgar was achieving a major performance in the capital where he had failed to establish himself all those years before.

But once again he had to accept the commercial realities: if the performance did not make a profit, Novellos insisted that he would have to underwrite some of the losses himself.

The performance was successful, but ticket sales were poor, and Elgar was thus required to stump up the equivalent of more than £3,000 in today's money, out of his own pocket to make up for redress.

Elgar's growing reputation as a composer hardly brought him in any further commercial gain.

His next large scale production – the cantata *'Caractacus'*, commissioned by the 1898 Leeds Festival, brought him a total of £12,000 in today's terms, half of that sum coming from the Festival and the other half coming from Novellos for the copyright. But this was scant reward for the months of hard work in writing it.

Furthermore, at Leeds he had interacted with other composers who were making a tidy living from their work – people like Parry and Stanford, and Sir Arthur Sullivan, the Chief Conductor at the Festival, who was the equivalent of a multi-millionaire from his compositions as well as his collaboration with Gilbert in the Savoy Operettas.

This hardly improved his mood regarding money – nor was it further improved by the fact that he had to go begging in order to receive what was agreed from the production.

As late as a month after the performance Elgar found himself reminding the publishers that they owed him and his librettist the money *'...Regarding 'Caractacus', you promised 10 gns [about £850] to Acworth [the librettist] and when you are putting fees straight I might have mine'*.

The aftermath left Elgar thoroughly depressed about his financial state. A month later, on December 17th, He wrote to his friend and mentor August Jaeger – who was also an employee of Novellos - expressing his despair:

'...for the last six weeks (about) I have been very sick at heart over music – the whole future seems so hopeless. I wrote to Mr L[ittleton] [Chairman of the firm] because I had talked to him of it previously & he does not reply; also I have asked how my egregious debt to the firm stands [i.e the money he owed them for the King Olaf performance] and they tell me nothing. Now I have worked steadily and honestly till I am offered all the festivals & then the firm seem to have had enough of me.

'I can quite understand that my big works don't pay -i.e. show any good return but I shd. have hoped that on artistic grounds the very small remuneration I ask shd. be forthcoming for things which at least interest the better portion of the musical public. No! The only suggestion made is that the Henry VIII dances [by Edward German] are the thing – now I can't write that sort of thing & my own heartfelt ideas are not wanted: why K[ing] Olaf should be worthless when it's done often is a mystery to me when things by, say, [Sir Alexander] MacKenzie, which are never touched, shd be good properties.

'You see I want so little: £300 [about £25,000 today] a year I must make, and that's all. Last year I subsisted on £200 [about £16,000 today]. It seems strange that a man who might do good work shd be absolutely stopped - but that's what it means.

'Now you see how things are, do not tell anyone all this or any of it. I did not intend to write as it may seem disloyal to the firm but apparently this is the end of all things, so it doesn't matter.'

Jaeger replied:

'England expects every man to do his duty and no musician in your great and glorious country has a greater duty to fulfil than you. So don't dare to talk about your new work being squashed. Nonsense! A day's attack of the blues due to a touch of indigestion or a blast of east wind will not drive away your desire, your

necessity which is to exercise those creative faculties which a kind providence has given you. Your time of universal recognition will come. You have virtually achieved more towards that in one year than others of the English composers in a decade.'

Fine and supportive words, no doubt. But Jaeger was basing his argument on an artistic dimension. Elgar on the other hand, was pleading for the kind of money which would make his effort worthwhile.

What Jaeger hadn't realised was that this period was a real crisis in his life - and one which might have ended with a decision to abandon composition altogether.

It was all very well Jaeger assuring him that all, one day, would be well, but this is an easy enough argument to put forward when, like Jaeger, you receive a steady salary. Elgar was having to live directly from the remuneration of his efforts, and to live with all the uncertainties that such a life created. Everything he produced had to 'sell', and that pressure alone created its own momentum.

By this time he had worked solidly for almost 10 years, and, as he said in his letter, made enormous financial sacrifices in order to try to establish himself as a composer. He had already seen his big commercial money-spinner *'Salut d'Amour'* slip through his fingers, while others reaped profits from his work, and had experienced the realities, and one might suggest, *insult*, of having to accept scant offers from the business world resulting in a financial return which was much less than he was hoping for. Time spent composing was time denied from teaching – and teaching, on the other hand, had provided him with a reasonably comfortable living. So was it worth considering abandoning composition and returning full time to his teaching ?

The sentiments expressed in Jaeger's letter and the suggestion that his mood was no more than *'a day's attack of the blues'*, has long given rise to a notion that Elgar suffered from mood-swings and possibly that he suffered from some sort of bi-polar condition.

I would argue that this was definitely not the case.

Such a suggestion ignores the underlying, and long standing, reasons for his depression, which can only be understood, in my humble submission, by anyone who has experienced the same financial traumas which naturally accompany the life of a freelance. The constant risks of failure. The feelings of rejection. The embarrassment and bitterness of knowing that you have undersold yourself. The lack of the sort of rewards you consider reasonable for your expertise and efforts. Coming up with a great creative idea and then having to stand by as it is torn apart by those from the world of commerce who you might regard as artistic Philistines, but who nevertheless have control over your financial future, and therefore you find yourself having to respect their opinions. The relentless requirement to make ends meet when the financial success of the next project is always in doubt, and having to go, cap-in-hand, to receive the money you had a reasonable belief you would receive months before.

Speaking as such a freelance myself, I can certainly fully understand why he was so depressed at this time – and it had absolutely nothing to do with any mental condition.

The evidence is in his letters. He was not receiving a steady salary from publishers, nor was he on any long standing retainer from concert promoters and the various festivals up and down the country that were showcasing his work. Neither did he have any substantial private family income to allow him to lead a comfortable life while composing.

Just as he had said in his letter to Jaeger, he had complied with everything which the publishers and the festivals had required of him, and it is interesting that he should feel that he had worked *'honestly'* during this time – in other words had not baulked when required to comply with their requirements.

Yet those *'requirements'* meant that he had been obliged to write particular types of works – part-songs for amateur choirs and choral cantatas for provincial festivals - and from comments in his letters they were obviously not the sort of works he had wished to write.

When Leeds had approached him for *'Caractacus'* for instance, he had commented: *'I hear that nothing save the merest accident will prevent my being asked to* *contribute a Cantata to the Leeds Fest[ival]: <u>I have hinted at other things</u> but it seems they wish a Cantata.'*

So by the end of 1898, it is reasonable to suppose that his assessment of his achievements after almost 10 years, was a career which had seen him producing works he didn't particularly wish to write, and remuneration far below what he had been expecting.

I am not at all surprised that he was naturally wondering whether it was worthwhile continuing.

In a letter to his friend and confident Nicholas Kilburn written shortly after the *'Caractacus'* production, in November 1898 he wrote this:

'I am doing nothing absolutely in the way of music - & don't want to - probably I shall have to begin to write again - Worcester, Norwich & Birmingham all ask me but silence 'pays' almost better than sound & I hesitate about casting myself into the whirlpool again: shall I?

Such sentiments were echoed in letters he wrote to Jaeger during this period:

'I'm really giving up all music & am refusing everything – I cannot afford to waste my precious few years of remaining outdoor life – so I fish, etc much better than your damned old blasted music' [September 1898]

'No – I'm not happy at all in fact never was more miserable in my life: I don't see that I've done any good at all: if I write a tune you all say it's commonplace – if I

don't, you all say it's rot – well, I've written Caractacus, earning thro' it 15shillings [about £60 today] a week while doing it and that's all – now if I will write any easy, small choral-society work for Birmingham, using the fest[ival] as an advert – your firm will be 'disposed to consider it ' – but my own natural bent I must choke off. No thank you – no more music for me – at present.' [October 20th 1898]

Four days after this letter he announced that he'd *'sketched a set of Variations'* for orchestra.

These were, of course, the *'Enigma Variations'* which were destined finally to put him on the international musical map – though, once again, his proposals for the work received lukewarm reaction from the publishers.

It is easy to understand their reluctance. It was the same situation he had encountered with *'Froissart'* 10 years earlier. They naturally wanted works which were popular, could be easily published and bought in volume.

Elgar's ideas of producing a complicated work for a very large orchestra which would not only be extremely expensive to print, but could only be performed by a handful of competent orchestras throughout the country, hardly seemed like a sensible business proposition.

The schism was thus: *he* was reluctant to write the sort of easily published material that they wanted – *they* were reluctant to take on the gamble of expensively producing the works Elgar had in mind.

From their point of view their attitude was logical. Music publishing is not the same animal as literature publishing. In the case of, say, a 50,000 word novel, the printing involved is a matter of typesetting . In those days it would have involved setting up pages of type. But as each copy of the book would have been identical, this was worth doing. An edition of many thousands of copies could thus be easily produced – becoming ever cheaper as each copy was printed.

The publication of music is much more complicated. In Elgar's day, the pages of music would have had to be engraved – a somewhat laborious and time consuming operation, particularly as each page has to be proofed and, if corrections were required, re-engraved. Furthermore, with a work such as 'The Enigma Variations' the individual parts for each instrument of the orchestra needed to be separately engraved, as well as all the pages of the complete, conductor's score. It was no simple task.

This division between Elgar and the publisher deepened as the weeks progressed and in early January 1899 he poured out his heart in this letter to his friend Nicholas Kilburn:

My dear Kilburn:

I am afraid you must have thought that silence at this time of the year foreboded evil or followed it. We have been thro' a time of much searching of heart with the result that I am going to write a little more music before going to my teaching: it seems ludicrous to think that the position I have striven for & in a great measure attained shd. be utterly & entirely useless from any practical point of view. But so it is: I have denied myself almost every pleasure - even a solitary cigar - & have subsisted on less wages than the merest clerk for three years & now although my 'things' are going on - more than anyone else's just now - my labour is in vain & the publishers only want me to use my position to advertise & sell - well, rot!

'So I have made up my mind to return to teaching - but - to avoid breaking my dear wife's heart I am going on once more - but without the spirit - it seems a wrecked life!

'I have completed, nearly, a set of variations for orchestra – but commercially nothing.'

Despite Novellos' reluctance, the 'Variations' *were* published and performed to great critical acclaim in June 1899.

But perhaps an indication of how Elgar felt about the whole business of music at this period of his career, can be found in the Italian quotation he wrote at the end of the score: '*Brama assai, poco spera e nulla chiede*'. Which translates to: '*He craves for much, he has little hope and asks for nothing.*'

And a stark reminder as to Novellos' enthusiasm at publishing his chosen style of composition can be gleaned from the fact that they paid him just 1gn [about £90] for the copyright, together with a scant agreement on any royalties.

A masterpiece which remains a favourite to this day in the concert halls around the world, was thus yet again given away for next to nothing. One wonders how much the publishers made from the *'Nimrod'* Variation alone in the 105 years which ensued before the work finally went out of copyright.

The anger which Elgar felt at his treatment over the Variations led him to offer his next work – the song cycle *'Sea Pictures'* to the rival firm of Boosey and Hawkes- who paid him £50 [more than £4,000 today]. They also paid him £100 [more than £8,000 today] for the copyright of the subsequent first two short *'Pomp and Circumstance Marches'* which appeared in 1901.

In between, he had written for the Birmingham Festival his choral masterpiece *'The Dream of Gerontius'* – again published by Novellos, who paid him the same amount – just £100 - for a work which had taken him virtually the whole year to compose.

Although matters changed somewhat in 1903 when his next work for the Birmingham Festival, *'The Apostles'*, where he received £1,000 [more than £80,000 today] – this was largely because J H Johnson, the Chairman of the Birmingham Festival Committee, took it upon himself to negotiate on Elgar's behalf. The difference between a negotiator who was well versed in business matters and Elgar acting on his own behalf was thus starkly exposed.

The performance of *'The Apostles'* elevated Elgar's status in the musical world, to the extent that plans were drawn up for a three day festival at the Royal Opera House, Covent Garden, devoted exclusively to Elgar's music – the first time in history that such an event had been given over to the works of a sole English composer.

Elgar had suddenly become a very lucrative business proposition, who, it was logical to suppose, could command the attention of a considerable number of commercial offers. He had already demonstrated his ability to sell his work to other publishers with *'Sea Pictures'* and the *'Pomp and Circumstance' Marches* – which had brought him in almost 150 times what Novellos had paid him for the copyright of the *'Enigma' Variations'*.

One might question at the wisdom therefore as to why Elgar in 1904, at such a time when his international prestige had been so firmly secured, and his abilities to secure much better commercial deals, that he agreed to enter into an *exclusive* publishing contract with Novellos.

It is even more remarkable to reflect that this *'contract'* amounted, in effect, to no more than a gentlemanly exchange of letters.

The first came from Alfred Littleton, Chairman of the firm which proposed royalties of 25% of the marked price of both choral and orchestral works. As far as advances were concerned, he said this: *'the question of payment down before royalties become due must I am afraid be left for arrangement in each individual case – but as we have now several precedents to go on I do not think this can cause any difficulty.'*

Littleton's letter also mentioned that the agreement would run for five years *'each of us having the right to give 12 months' notice of our wish to cancel it at the end of five years or any future date...'*

Elgar replied that he had spoken to several of his friends about such an arrangement and they had *'strongly dissuaded him from accepting it'*.

However, astonishingly one might suggest, he then clearly ignored their advice and agreed to the whole thing via the following letter:

'In reference to your very kind letters & the propositions contained in them I write now to accept your offer. That is to say in future for five years certain & after that time so long as we may wish – the engagement that is, to be terminated by six months' notice on either side, I send you everything I write...& you pay me a royalty of one fourth of the marked price & a sum 'down' for new works such as you have been in the habit of paying for in addition to royalties or on account of royalties...'

It would be natural to assume that such an exchange of letters would be merely the opening gambit – the sort of thing which is termed today *'heads of agreement'* – i.e a broad outline of what each party wanted and offered in return. Such a procedure would then lead to a formal contract being drawn up by lawyers, amounting to forensic examination of the agreement, clauses to deal with details, and then signed off, with witnesses present.

This does not appear to be the case. Elgar's letter, was kept by Novellos in an envelope marked 'Elgar's Publishing Contract' – so we must assume that this was, in effect, the only legal arrangement between both parties, and that this was the document that covered the publication and performance of most of Elgar's great works for the following years. These included the big choral oratorio *'The Kingdom' 'Introduction and Allegro for Strings'*, the *First Symphony*, the *Violin Concerto* and the *Second Symphony,* plus several other lesser pieces.

It seems remarkable that Elgar would agree to such an arrangement without consulting a lawyer. Perhaps he did – and perhaps such a person may have been one of those who argued against him accepting the arrangement - but there is no evidence of this – and anyway if such legal advice had been offered, it was obviously ignored. Perhaps he assumed that the one year he spent as a solicitor's apprentice all those years before had taught him all he needed to know about contract law. That is certainly the view of at least one of his subsequent biographers.

But when you see the contracts drawn up for individual productions by other artists – often running into several closely typed pages, each of which is carefully signed off, initialled, amended with initials and finally signed off with witnesses by both parties - the brevity and legal deficiencies in this arrangement are, to be frank, mind boggling.

Anyone with even the most rudimentary understanding of contracts can see the yawning legal gaps in this arrangement.

Elgar agreed to *'25% of the marked price'* as a royalty – but there is no indication as to what that *'marked price'* might be – nor whether, in the event of different scales of *'marked price'* that royalty percentage might be varied. There was also no indication as to whether this royalty amounted to *all* sales. In the event of a runaway success such as Schotts had on their hands with *'Salut d'Amore'*, would this generous-sounding royalty still obtain, or would there be a sliding scale ?

There is no indication of any yearly review within the contract period, no indication of what Elgar might receive from international sales, no indication of any remuneration for arrangements of his works, no indication of *when* Elgar might expect to be paid, and no indication of what redress Elgar might expect if Novellos failed to honour the 'contract' – or indeed, failed to pay him on time.

They had also indicated a notice period of 12 months. Elgar said six months in his letter – but again, there is no indication that this was agreed by both parties, and, as we shall see, this led to perhaps the most embarrassing episode in Elgar's career.

I suppose Elgar was initially pleased with the arrangement. His success was such at this period that he had achieved what might be described today as *'rock star'* status. Every new work he produced was greeted with adulation by the audiences up and down the country. Ticket sales were oversubscribed.

Indeed, it was noted by some critics at the time that while Elgar's works were achieving such audience acclaim, they questioned whether the audience reaction was more to do with Elgar's newly established *'celebrity'* status, rather than any true appreciation of the quality of what they were hearing.

As one very perceptive critic observed when *'The Kingdom'* was first performed in 1906: *'We found the usual throng of eager, expectant, gorgeously attired people, all trying to look as if they had written the work themselves, and some of them almost succeeding. After all, people do not, as a rule, pay one guinea [about £85 today] and costs merely to say 'I was there' so I expect there is something genuine in a festival audience with their devout attention to their vocal scores and their charming air of detachment from all worldly matters.*

'The whole scene was elevating; the whole atmosphere was charged with electricity. One noted so many well-known types. The old Festival Stager, quiet, composed, absorbed, score in hand, ostentatiously familiar. The ardent amateur, busy with pencil notes and ready with a 'Jaeger' label for every tune. The diffident but earnest

novice, who strives to emulate the old stager and the ardent amateur, and very much wishes that he knew what that clever Mr Jaeger means by his charming analysis. The opulent night-seer and lion-hunter, who goes to a festival as he goes to Madam Tussaud's and who is quite aware that both are dependent on him for their very existence.

'The critic with a well-chosen manner indicative in being engaged in assimilating every subject under the sun, except music. The great musician, oblivious of all other types, and cognisant only of a very small and very select coterie surrounded by a sort of mental halo, only to be approached upon bended knees. They were all there...'

From Elgar's point of view the agreed arrangement of this *'publishing contract'* had its advantages. It meant he didn't have to bother anymore with any day-to-day business negotiations – he could just get on with the adulation of the crowds, the writing of the works, and the rest of his life. But one might argue that this was such a thoroughly casual attitude that it would allow more hard-nosed business people to walk all over him financially – which in all honesty they did.

From Novellos' point of view, they had tied down what might have been considered a *'hot property'* in Elgar who was riding at the peak of public adulation, sales were booming, and the *'contract'* provided a very simple set of requirements, which, had it been scrutinised by a lawyer on Elgar's behalf would almost certainly never have been agreed to.

Things went on swimmingly for a number of years. The *First Symphony,* was performed almost 100 times in its first year alone, and the *Violin Concerto* premiered to great acclaim with the world's greatest violinist Fritz Kreisler taking the solo part.

Matters took a downward course however, with the production of the *Second Symphony* in 1911.

Its complex structure, baffling third movement, and quiet reflective ending, struck a different tone with critics and audiences alike who had been expecting a triumphant work full of the sort of Elgarian energy displayed in the previous *symphony* and *concerto*. It was deemed not a success, and subsequent performances were so little attended that Elgar, who conducted the first and two later performances, decided to forego any conducting fees as a result.

Such a sudden stuttering of the roller-coaster success of the previous years brought Elgar to review the whole status of his contract situation with Novellos and he wrote indicating that he wished the arrangement to be terminated. He wrote to them thus:

'Enclosed I send formal receipt for the annual royalty acct & some performing fees. The account is very disappointing & I must ask you to accept this as notice to terminate the agreement existing between us as to

publishing – I believe 12 months' notice is required but I have not Mr Littleton's letter here which forms the agreement.

'I need not say that I send this notice with very great regret but I see no other course open to me.'

This may have been a genuine feeling of realisation that the *'contract'* had not brought him in the sort of rewards he had expected. However, there is always the possibility that Elgar was attempting in a rather ham-fisted way to achieve better contract terms. In other words, he might have been bluffing in the hope that his status might have brought a reaction from Novellos that he was far too good a property to let go and therefore might have offered better terms. A subsequent letter, as we shall see, suggests this.

However, it must have come to him as a shock when he received *by return of post* the following from an unnamed source at the publishers – the letter was merely signed *'Novello & Co'* – though it was actually written by Henry Clayton, Director and Company Secretary, a man who could certainly be described in business terms as 'hard-nosed':

'Dear Sir

'We are favoured with your letter of the 27th inst signifying your desire to terminate the publishing agreement which you made with us in 1904. We need not say with what regret we have received this intimation of your decision in the matter.

'We have consulted the letters which constitute the agreement between us & find that Mr Littleton's letter of April 14th 1904 suggested a notice of 12 months' on either side. Your letter of June 7th 1904 however, in repeating the terms, mentions six months' notice on either side. The point however is immaterial; as to restrict your freedom of action in any way is the last thing we should wish. Please therefore entirely disregard the question of notice.'

The terse nature of this letter was nothing short of brutal. Instead of pleading with him to reconsider, and perhaps offer better terms to encourage him to think again, they not only acquiesced to his demand, but furthermore dispensed with any notice period. He could go, and today!

Such a reply must have shocked him, but to make matters worse, his repost was to write a letter, to of all people, the Chairman Alfred Littleton personally.

'I am very grateful to you for your kind letter about the termination of our agreement. I want to tell you at once that I have made no other arrangements and have not contemplated making any. I am not dissatisfied with the firm, although there are some minor points we might have adjusted- not worth considering really apart from the big question which is as follows.

'I have never deceived myself as to my true commercial value & see that everything of mine, as I have often said, dies a natural death; - if you look at the accounts you will see that a new thing of mine 'lasts' about a year & then

dies & is buried in the mass of English music: under these inevitable circumstances it seems to me that the royalty system we adopted in 1904 cannot really be satisfactory to either of us. I am now well on in years & have to consider a 'move' & make a new home – under the depressing state of my music I have to reconsider this entirely & shall probably go abroad or to a cottage in the country & leave the musical world entirely.

'My reference to a 'sum down' refers to the fact that other publishers have offered me in the past, a substantial sum for a new work: under the present strain this wd. suit me better & there is no reason, that I can see, that your firm shd. not do this: only I have no work on hand & contemplate no large work in the future – I may think of large works but I shall not write them; to write them is labour lost. I hope I may see you. I write this hastily to assure you that nothing was farther from my mind than any 'break' with the firm except that the royalty system does not seem to suit my needs: I thought a formal notice was absolutely necessary for the firm as a Ltd Company – Also the notice (12 months) which the firm waives if I like, had better be adhered to.'

This letter more than any other I have seen over the years betrays Elgar's naivety in the world of business.

Apart from declaring that he had had no intention to *'break'* the contract when only a few days before he had written giving formal notice exactly to that effect, there are a number of aspects which become immediately apparent.

In the first instance, was it really *wise* for him to write to, of all people, the Chairman of such an important publishing company, with whom, by this time, he had had an exclusive contract for *seven years*, and declare that his works were of no true commercial value, that everything he wrote *'dies a natural death'*, and that inspection of the accounts would show that a new work from his pen *'only lasts for a year'* and is then *'buried in the mass of English music'* ?

Furthermore, was it wise to state that anyway he was thinking of giving up the whole thing, retiring to some country retreat and although he might contemplate writing again, would not do so ?

It is also worthy of note, that while he had received a letter that same day pointing out that he had originally asked for a six months' notice period, but as far as they were concerned he could go that very day without any notice period at all, he somehow felt that he could personally re-instate a 12 months' notice period – which in the first place he had never agreed to, and moreover had originally insisted on a six months' notice period - claiming that it was his right to do so.

In the event, Novellos tacitly agreed to the 12 months' notice period, but unfortunately for Elgar, this was to come back to haunt him the following year.

In that year, 1912, Elgar was approached by the powerful Stoll Theatre Syndicate to write the music for an *'Imperial Masque'* they were arranging to celebrate George V's visit to India where he was to be crowned Emperor. The work was to be staged at their flagship theatre, the London Coliseum.

The work comprised a number of elements, all of which were very much the sort of thing which were main-stream business for a firm such as Novellos, including individual songs, choruses and orchestral music - all of which could be published individually, as well as offered in piano and small ensemble arrangements, with considerable sale potential, given the national mood at the event. Naturally they had every reason to believe that they would get the publishing rights. Elgar even wrote to them saying that he had set up a meeting for them with Bernie Shelton, the Syndicate's Manager, and producer of the *Masque*, to discuss terms.

He must have been somewhat surprised when he received a letter from Novellos, once again written by Henry Clayton, following that meeting. After reporting that they had offered to publish the music he continued ' *Mr Shelton however has evidently put an entirely different construction on your wishes in the matter. He absolutely declined to discuss the business on the basis of publication by Novellos. He said that his Principal had already made other arrangements, that the particular kind of music in question was not in our line at all, that our contract with you had come to an end and that we had no locus standi !!*

'*When we demurred to his last two pronouncements he informed us that at all events we were out of court on the question of the existence of the contract on which we were presuming to rely and that he had seen our letter to you waiving our right to the 12 months' notice for which our contract provides.*

'*As he had informed us that he had seen our letter to you waiving the right to notice, we thought it was time that we showed him that we are not the unprincipled people which he must have thought us to be after our Chairman's emphatic statement to him a few weeks ago that the contract was still in force.*

'*So we showed him your letter to our Chairman of June 30th ult which concludes with the following remark:-*

"*Also the notice (12 months) which the Firm waives if I like, had better be adhered to.*"

'*No doubt you had forgotten the fact that you had written that letter; for Mr Shelton was evidently much surprised and having read your remarks & having taken note of the date of the letter, he admitted that that letter put a very different complexion on the case as it affects us.*

'*We told Mr Shelton that, although our rights were still regulated by the Contract made in 1904 we were nevertheless willing to discuss the business on the lines suggested to you by our Chairman.*

'He, however, declined to discuss matters with us at all, and he left saying he would report to his Principal and would leave us to settle matters with you.

'To that we replied that that would be entirely in accordance with our views & would be only what was customary in our transactions with you...'

Elgar's reply amounted to a grovelling apology, saying that he hadn't realised the contract extension *which he had asked for* was still in place, and adding that he didn't think the music was in Novellos' line at all.

As a P.S. he added : *'I know of no arrangements having been made with other publishers.'*

If this was the case, it was certainly very odd, as within days it was announced that the publishing rights were given to the firm of Enoch & Sons – worth around £50,000 in today's money.

From the evidence of the correspondence, Elgar seemed very selective in his memory as well as his conversations with both parties. Shelton had apparently seen Novellos' letter to Elgar waiving the notice period – this could only have been shown to them by Elgar himself.

He had received this letter on the day he had written his own to Littleton, yet did not appear to have kept a copy – or at least conveniently *'forgot'* that he had written such a letter requiring an extension to the contract.

It may seem unkind to Elgar to suggest that he thought he might 'get away' with securing lucrative business from the Stoll Syndicate while knowing that he was effectively still under contract to Novellos. It may also seem unkind to suggest that his handling of the whole business, to put it mildly, was somewhat cavalier. But the evidence certainly points in that direction. In the event, he was dealing with two powerful business operations – and people who made sure they kept copies of correspondence, checked out their dealings through legal advisors, and above all, knew chapter and verse about contract law.

Elgar was in a very difficult position, and today might have faced legal action from both Novellos, for breach of contract, and the Stoll Syndicate, for deception. Thankfully for him, this was a much more gentlemanly age, and eventually Novellos relented and withdrew from the whole business.

Their letter displayed however, their feelings in the matter quite succinctly:

'Dear Sir

Having now carefully considered the question of the publication of the music which you have written for the Indian Masque, about to be produced at the Coliseum, we have decided, if in your opinion it is in your interest that the work should be published elsewhere, not to interfere with any other scheme of publication, which you have in view, by asserting our right to the work under the terms of the existing Contract.

'We cannot help expressing our great regret that you should have formed that opinion, but, having done so, will you please consider that as far as we are concerned you have a free hand in the matter.

With Compliments.'

Thus ended what could have been a very damaging episode in Elgar's life, brought about entirely by own his naivety in the world of business.

Once the contract had run out, he of course had the opportunity of seeking publication wherever he wished, but for some reason still came back to Novellos.

In this context one further episode is worthy of mention.

In February 1914, he wrote to Novellos offering them five part-songs. These were among his best works in this genre and included *'The Shower'*, *'The Fountain'*, *'Love's Tempest'* and, perhaps his finest, *'Death on the Hills'*.

He asked for an advance of 125gns and an immediate royalty of 25% of the marked price. The advance was equivalent in today's money of more than £10,000. Perhaps the realisation of what he could earn from his theatrical experiences had finally taught him a lesson.

This may or may not have been the case, but at the very least it prompted an immediate and almost desperate response.

Augustus Littleton, brother of the Chairman who by this time was taking more control of the company's affairs cabled immediately on reading Elgar's offer: *'Must agree Elgar's terms'*.

This was backed up with a more comprehensive letter commenting: *'I don't think we ought to hesitate a moment. The price is high amounting to extortion, but the point is that plenty of other houses would jump at the stuff at the price...this is a very different matter to the Indian ballet. Here we are on our own ground and if the partsongs catch on we shall make money, anyway we cannot afford to throw up the sponge just yet. The future must take care of itself, and if Elgar repeats himself, which he won't in his own interest just yet, we must consider each case on its merits.'*

Littleton then demanded that the published versions should carry the high price of 6d [about £2 today] adding: *'The higher price won't stop the Part songs going if they catch on, if people grumble we must quietly let them know that the higher rate is owing to the composer's greed.'*

He finally concluded with a sentence which, in effect, summed up their attitude to Elgar's output at this time:

'I don't want any more Elgar symphonies or concertos, but am ready to take as many part songs as he can produce even at extortionate rates. If they don't show an immediate return of the money they ought to prove good capital investment. But each case wants individual consideration.'

This final aspect sums up the fundamental difficulties which Elgar had throughout his composing career. He had wished to write music in a particular way – he had wished to produce orchestral music on the grand scale, and doubtless had ideas for many more works than he actually produced.

But *his* ideas and intentions ran counter-clockwise to the business requirements of publishers and performers alike. Publishing his works was expensive, and in many respects his music was too difficult for the competence of performers at the time.

Ironically this was also the case even with Mozart, who's publisher at one point asked him not to write works he had initially been commissioned by them to compose, because they felt his music was too difficult to perform and therefore the music was unsaleable.

After 1914 the only works Elgar produced which stand alongside his great achievements of the previous years were three chamber works and the 'cello concerto – written during a 'swan-song' period in 1918/19, and which were to prove to be the very last great works he ever completed.

Shortly afterwards, in early 1920, his composing career came to a virtual full stop with the death of his wife Alice. She had been the rock upon which his career had been based, and she it was who had been the constant impetus for him to compose at all.

With her death that impetus had gone. The popular belief is that he was so grief stricken at her death that he decided never to compose major works again. To a certain extent this may be the case, but perhaps by this time, he had formed the view that it was hardly worth carrying on anyway.

Shortly after the first performance of the 'Cello Concerto, and only a few weeks before Alice's death, he had written the following to his friend Nicholas Kilburn, with a clear reference to his feelings about the financial aspects of his career:

My pen has been idle for months – so much the better for prosperity and posterity...

So in other words even at the end of his mainstream composing career he carried the belief that his works were hardly worth it both in terms of artistic merit and even more so in financial terms.

In the aftermath of Alice's death, there was more than sufficient evidence to confirm this view. On 10 June 1921, Henry Clayton wrote to him sending the account for the Royalties on sales for the previous *five years* of a wide range of Elgar's music, as well as many arrangements of his works. It amounted to a total of £256.9s.7d [about £7,500].

Consequently he added:

'Of course the valuation of these Royalties is a pure speculation – or a gamble – as owing to the varying

fashions, tastes and conditions, no one can say what the future is to be.

But three of us have carefully gone into the matter & we have formulated ideas as to what we can & ought to pay for the surrender of the Royalties in question & without further explanation that sum is £500 [about £14,500] for the lot!!

Elgar's reply left no doubt as to his mood at that time:

'I wish the firm could see its way to buy me out entirely; I never really belonged to the musical world – I detest my slightest necessary connection with it & shall be glad to have done with it and get back to my (deceased) dogs and horses!

Had matters been different – had Elgar had the fundamental capital and steady income to be able to compose at will, or had the necessary business acumen in his financial dealings with publishers, we may have seen many more symphonies and concertos, large scale orchestral works and even operas from his pen. He had wished to write at least one opera all his life.

It is also possible that if he had been so unbending in his artistic attitudes and faced up to commercial realities - writing more commercially popular works along the lines of the output of contemporaries such as Edward German, he might have derived sufficient reward to allow him to compose more of the works, such as the symphonies and concertos, which he wished to write.

But his naivety in business coupled with his somewhat lowly financial base meant that he had to rely on the profits from his efforts and in that regard he had to conform to the dictates of business

Elgar's business dealings were, to sum up, chaotic to say the least, and guaranteed that he never fully realised the full extent of what he might have received from his efforts over the years.

When he died, in 1934 he left a nett estate of £9,104 – about £450,000 in today's money. Or just about what Haydn Wood made in royalties from just one of his songs.

LAND OF HOPE AND GLORY

'Land of Hope and Glory' is perhaps Elgar's best known work - it is also one which divides opinion throughout the world.

To some it is the alternative National Anthem – a song which should be respected as embodying everything which is British. But to others it epitomises a celebration of an Empire long consigned to the past, and in its most disputed lines *'wider still and wider, shall thy bounds be set'* an aspiration for a restoration of colonial domination.

Elgar is said to have eventually come to hate it – though this may be anecdotal, and it *was* the tune of 'Land of Hope and Glory' which he conducted on his famous Pathé News film when he opened the Abbey Road Studios in London in the 1930s.

If, in fact, he did come to hate it – and to be fair, there is no firm proof that he did - the reason was probably because the song had morphed into something which he had never intended – and indeed it is debateable whether Elgar actually wrote what we now know as the popular song which is sung with such vigour on occasions such as the 'Last Night of the Proms'.

The history of the piece dates back to 1899, at a time when he was the rising star in the musical world. His reputation had soared through his large scale choral works which had received growing approval. And just at the same time that he was completing the 'Enigma Variations' – the work which was to place him at the forefront of international fame - the Worcester Festival asked him to write a symphony.

Elgar liked the idea, and decided to choose the subject of General Charles Gordon as a narrative for the work.

Gordon, a British General and Administrator was sent to Khartoum in the Sudan in 1884, after a serious revolt had broken out, led by a Muslim religious leader and self-proclaimed Mahdi named Muhammad Ahmad.

Gordon's instructions were to secure the evacuation of loyal soldiers and civilians and to depart with them. In defiance of those instructions, after evacuating about 2,500 civilians he retained a smaller group of soldiers and non-military men.

Besieged by the Mahdi's forces, Gordon organised a citywide defence lasting almost a year that gained him the admiration of the British public, but not of the government, which had wished him not to become entrenched. Only when public pressure to act had become irresistible did the government, with reluctance, send a relief force, but it arrived two days after the city had fallen and Gordon had been killed.

Gordon's death caused national grief in Britain, and he was quickly revered as a martyr – not only because he was known to be a very devout Christian, but also because the legend grew that he had met his death in full ceremonial dress, facing his enemy armed only with supreme courage. It was a Christian symbol which was not lost on the public mind.

When the relief force arrived, they also found a copy of Cardinal John Henry Newman's long narrative poem concerning the passage of the soul from this world into heaven, *'The Dream of Gerontius'*. Gordon had marked certain passages in the copy they found which indicated that he knew he was going to make the ultimate sacrifice of his life but was facing it with courage and fortitude.

Such was the public feeling at the time, that publishers produced copies of the poem containing the 'Gordon markings', and one of these copies was given to Elgar as a wedding present when he had married in 1889. Eleven years later he set the poem to music in one of his greatest masterpieces.

So it seemed appropriate for Elgar to base his intended symphony on the legend of Gordon and he set about his task with enthusiasm.

However, matters did not run smoothly, and like many projects which Elgar had worked on throughout his life, the symphony was never completed.

At the time, Elgar allowed it to be suggested that the reason why he did not complete the symphony was because the Worcester Festival Committee hadn't offered him enough money.

The Daily News, for example, under the headline *'The Payment of Composers'*, commented: *'It is becoming more and more the question how much longer the urgent claims of art are to be sacrificed to those of charity. The* question has indeed, at this festival, arisen in another form. In the earlier prospectuses, a symphony or some important composition of that character was announced from the pen of Mr Edward Elgar.

'It was afterwards withdrawn, and the reason, as I am credibly informed, is that the committee declined to pay an adequate fee for it, thinking British musicians should contribute their brainwork gratuitously. This, I believe, is the beginning of a campaign on the part of British composers which may have far-reaching consequences upon our annual festivals. Composers notoriously are not the wealthiest members of the community and they, at least, fail to see why they alone of the professional musicians engaged at the festival should be expected to work for nothing, in order that the funds available for charity may be thus unfairly augmented.'

And the Glasgow Herald amplified: *'Mr Elgar is just now extremely popular with his brother musicians owing to the withdrawal of his promised Symphony from the Worcester Festival on the ground that the committee were not willing to pay properly for his work, £100* [about £8,000 in today's money] *being the sum mentioned. Mr Elgar, it is true, is a man of considerable private means* [no, he wasn't !] *but it is claimed that men of fortune are often the readiest to work for nothing and thus spoil the markets. Besides a poorer composer might have been afraid to take so strong a stand, lest he might be boycotted by festival committees. The foreign contributor to English festivals is invariably well paid, for the intelligent foreigner has a very healthy objection to working for nothing.'*

The Worcester Festival, however, reacted angrily to these suggestions and in a letter to a local paper, T L Claughton, Chairman of the Festival Committee stated angrily : *'My attention having been drawn to a paragraph which, I am informed, has been copied into many newspapers, stating that the withdrawal of Mr Elgar's promised Symphony from the Worcester Festival was due to the fact that the "Committee were not willing to pay properly for his work, £100 being the sum mentioned". Will you allow me as a member of the Committee and having acted as Chairman at its meetings, to give the most unqualified contradiction to this statement? No proposal of the kind was brought before the Committee and no such sum was ever mentioned there as a condition of the fulfilment of Mr Elgar's promise.'*

Despite the fact that the symphony had not been completed, Elgar nevertheless had produced various sketches and themes which he intended to use. One of these was a tune which was noble and stately and it is logical to assume that this was intended as the main theme evoking the character of Gordon himself. Elgar raved about it saying it would *'knock 'em flat when they hear it'*. It was also a tune which he described as one *'which only comes once in a lifetime'*. But, alas, it was never to be heard in his 'Gordon' Symphony.

Matters turned in a different direction when in 1901- and by this time he was regarded as by far the most important living British composer - he was asked to produce some new music for a friend, Alfred Rodewald, of the Liverpool Orchestral Society, and he came up with the idea of writing two military marches – which we know today as the first two of the *Pomp and Circumstance Marches*.

And in the first of these, he incorporated the famous tune, originally intended for the Gordon Symphony, which we easily recognise today as the tune of *'Land of Hope and Glory'*.

The first performance of the two marches, at Liverpool on October 19th 1901, caused a sensation. They struck an immediate accord with the Liverpool public, not only because the music provoked such a reaction, but also because at this time the country was still fighting the Boer War in South Africa. There were many young men from the area who were fighting, to the extent that the famous 'Kop' end at Liverpool's Anfield Stadium is named after Spion Kop – one of the worst battles to take place there.

The 'Gordon tune' which Elgar had incorporated in the first march was seen as a great hymn of triumph as the victorious army came home unscathed, as one contemporary review commented:

'...all is bustle and excitement as of an army marching gaily homeward knowing its work well done. Then in the trio [i.e. the 'Gordon' tune] *and the coda we seem to see a triumphal progress through a city 'all on fire with sun and cloth of gold' amid the blare of festal trumpets and the shouts of a nation making holiday'.*

A few days later, the marches were repeated at the Promenade Concerts in London, conducted by their founder Henry Wood, and caused an even bigger sensation. As Wood later recalled: *'The people simply rose and yelled. I had to play it again – with the same result; in fact they refused to let me go on with the programme. After considerable delay, while the audience roared its applause, I went off and fetched Harry Dearth who was to sing 'Hiawatha's Vision'; but they would not listen. Merely to restore order I played the march a third time. And that, I might say, was the one and only time in the history of the Promenade Concerts that an orchestral item was accorded a double encore.'*

Earlier that year Queen Victoria had died, and Edward VII acceded to the Throne. The Coronation was planned for the summer of 1902, and as part of the celebrations, the Royal Opera House, Covent Garden, organised a gala concert which was to feature excerpts from various operas, performed by some of the finest singers in the world.

Elgar was asked to produce a new choral work which would act as the first item on the programme, and he came up with the idea of a seven movement piece, called *'The Coronation Ode'* which would end in a grand hymn celebrating the new monarchy.

The librettist he chose to work with was Arthur Benson, son of a former Archbishop of Canterbury, and a Master at Eton College.

At this time Benson, now a largely forgotten figure, was a well-known poet, author and literary reviewer, and when it came to writing the words for the final hymn of triumph, he came up with the idea of celebrating both the past and the future.

The 64 years of the reign of Queen Victoria had certainly been a golden era which had seen huge technological, scientific, and artistic developments – as well as expansion of an Empire around the world.

These were the days of Isambard Kingdom Brunel, George and Robert Stephenson, Michael Faraday, the Great Exhibition, Dickens, Browning, Thomas Hardy, Wordsworth and Coleridge, J M W Turner, the Pre-Raphaelites and the rest. A truly golden age of technical, scientific and artistic development.

At the time, there was no reason to believe that the era of the past would not extend into the future, so Benson's idea was to celebrate a land of *hope*, for the future, and *glory*, in the achievements of the past.

Benson crafted the words, and it was suggested that Elgar should consider using the *'Gordon'* tune as the main theme of this hymn of triumph and celebration. After all, it had proved so incredibly popular at its debuts in Liverpool and London.

It is somewhat open to debate as to who actually suggested it. Some say it was the King himself, while others claim it was the leading contralto singer of the time, Dame Clara Butt, who saw the opportunity of such a hymn becoming a popular ballad.

Whatever the explanation, Elgar did use the tune - much to the annoyance of his friend and mentor August Jaeger who wrote to him : '...*I say you will have to write another tune for the 'Ode' in place of the March Tune. I have been trying much to fit words to it; that drop to E & the bigger drop afterwards are quite impossible in singing ANY words to them. They sound downright vulgar: just try it. The effect is fatal. No you must write a new tune to the words & not fit the words to this tune.*'

Elgar, for his part, ignored the advice and so *'Land of Hope and Glory'* was born – though at this stage it was somewhat different to the version which is sung today.

In the first place, this was a choral setting of the tune, with parts for soloists, and as such it differed radically from a simple ballad.

But additionally, the words which Benson wrote for this version were also different.

Benson's original version went like this:

'Land of Hope and Glory

Mother of the Free

How shall we extol thee

Who are born of thee

Truth and right and freedom

Each a holy gem

Stars in solemn brightness

Weave thy diadem'

You cannot escape the fact that these words, had they been left in the version which is sung today, would hardly have caused the controversy which has raged over the piece for all these years. They celebrate what we are proud to call *'British Values'* – freedom of expression, truth and human rights.

So what happened to the words – and why were they changed into the version which some consider notorious – celebrating the expansion of Empire and colonial domination ?

The explanation is a tale of woe which left neither Elgar nor Benson unscathed.

In the first place, the *'Coronation Ode'* never received its first performance at the Gala Concert.

Despite the fact that Elgar was given what must have constituted a huge budget to stage the piece, and a free hand to choose what forces he wished to perform it – and those included his favourite choir from Sheffield, the Band of the Coldstream Guards, and four of the finest soloists in the world including the legendary Dame Nellie Melba – the whole concert was called off.

Unfortunately, the King fell dangerously ill, had to undergo an emergency operation and the Coronation was postponed.

Elgar, for his part, was not phased. In fact, in a letter he wrote to a friend, he appeared to be relieved: *'...Don't for heaven's sake sympathise with me – I don't care a tinker's damn! It gives me three blessed sunny days in my own country (for which I thank God or the Devil) instead of stewing in town. My own interest in the thing ceased, as usual, when I had finished the manuscript.*

'I was biking out in Herefordshire yesterday & the news reached me at a little roadside pub: I said 'Give me another pint of cider'. I'm deadly sorry for the King – but that's all...'

The work finally had its first performance in Sheffield the following October as part of a concert featuring other works and has rarely been performed since.

However, the tune was still resonating widely with the public, and Benson's words seemed to create a rousing sentiment at a time when there was so much change taking place. The war was also coming to an end.

So the publishers decided to exploit the general mood and issue it as a popular ballad – using the tune unchanged from its original appearance as part of the Pomp and Circumstance March.

The words, however, were considered a stumbling block as they had been written for performance to celebrate the King's Coronation, and the feeling was that a popular ballad might have a longer life after that event.

So the publishers approached Benson and asked him to re-write the words. When the request came forth, it coincided with another major event – the death of that colonial grandee Cecil Rhodes, who left a huge bequest to the nation for the specific purpose of expansion of the Empire in Africa. So Benson latched on to the popular mood and substituted

Truth and right and freedom
Each a holy gem
Stars in solemn brightness
Weave thy diadem'

with the fateful lines:

'Wider still and wider
Shall thy bounds be set
God who made thee mighty
Make thee mightier yet.'

And it was this version which was sung at a sell-out popular concert by Dame Clara Butt, and which launched the song into immortality.

Elgar, for his part, had little say over the decision. He had sold the copyright of the tune when the Pomp and Circumstance Marches were first published, and of course he had not written the words and therefore had no copyright control over how they were changed.

Some years later, when the First World War broke out, Benson was asked to change the words again so that the song could be used as a rousing rallying hymn for the war effort.

Significantly Elgar wrote to him and demanded that the *'Wider still and Wider'* lines be deleted saying that they had lost their context by that time.

'Of course', he wrote, *'Wider Still and Wider'* should come out – it is liable to be misunderstood now.'

As a result, Benson's second re-write of his words went like this:

'Land of Hope and Glory

Mother of the free

How shall we uphold thee

Who are born of thee?

Gird thee well for battle,

Bid thy hosts increase,

Stand for faith and honour

Smite for truth and peace.'

Once again, Benson had struck a notion that we would describe today as *'British values'* of striving for faith, honour, truth and peace, but just as his first attempt for use in the *'Coronation Ode'* these words remain unknown today – and it is the *'Cecil Rhodes'* version which is now sung up and down the country and which is the subject of much hearty patriotic singing on the occasion of the Last Night of the Proms.

Yet, despite all its flag-waving popularity *'Land of Hope and Glory'* did little for Benson. He may have written the words of what is unquestionably one of the most well-known songs in the English language, but he is hardly known today and if asked to name the author of those words, few would ever mention him – opting most of the time to name Rudyard Kipling in that role.

As for Elgar, it has hung around the neck of his reputation like the proverbial albatross on the shoulders of Coleridge's Ancient Mariner, creating an impression that he was nothing more than a tub-thumping jingoistic composer of nationalist music.

It is arguable, however, that he never wrote 'Land of Hope and Glory' in the form for which he is so heavily criticised today. After all, he never sanctioned the words which were applied to his tune when it was released as a popular ballad. *His* tune had merely been part of an orchestral march written long before the words were ever conceived, and later incorporated into a choral piece written for a specific occasion of national celebration.

But perhaps, there is a final irony in the story of Elgar's tune.

When, in 1905, he received an Honorary Doctorate of Music from Yale University in America, the ceremony featured an orchestra playing some of Elgar's music as a preamble to the award being made.

One of the pieces which was featured was the *'Land of Hope and Glory'* tune. On hearing it, the University authorities were so impressed with it as a solemn melody which seemed to fit the importance of the occasion that they decided to adopt it for subsequent graduation ceremonies. Other Universities and colleges across the United States followed suit.

So to this day, the place where more than any other you might hear Elgar's Boer War marching song, seen by so many as the evocation of British Colonialism, is the very country that fought a war in order to free itself of that self-same colonial Empire !

THE ENIGMA VARIATIONS

The 'Enigma Variations' is perhaps Elgar's most internationally well-known work.

It dates from 1898/9, and is said to have been completed in just two months. When it was first performed at a concert in London in the summer of 1899 it created a sensation which immediately catapulted Elgar into the realms of international stardom. It also marked the beginning of his most creative period, which was to last for the next 20 years.

But at the time he was writing it, his general mood was at a particularly low ebb. This was a crisis point in his life which was so serious that had the *'Variations'* not been a success, there is a case for believing that he might have given up serious composition altogether.

The problem lay in the fact that although he had achieved great success throughout the 1890s with a succession of choral works, composed for the various festivals held in mainly industrial centres throughout the country, he had the feeling that his growing fame was not rewarding him financially, and that this had held him back from composing the sort of music he wished to write.

As we have seen, his preferred medium – and where his true genius lay – was not the sort of festival choral works which had hitherto been the hallmark of his career but orchestral music on a grand scale.

Unfortunately, the main vehicle for new music at the latter part of the 19th century *were* the festivals which mainly showcased choral music, blending the great choral masterpieces of Bach, Handel, Mendelssohn and the rest with new works by contemporary composers.

From the business point of view, such works were favoured by publishers and the festival organisers. Large choirs meant large potential attendances from families and friends of performers. Large choirs also meant large sales of sheet music to the performers – and often individual items from the works – such as songs or choruses – could be published separately and thus create an even wider sale.

Large scale, purely orchestral works were a completely different proposition. Printing the parts for each orchestral performer was expensive, and, when it came to the sort of complicated pieces Elgar may have had in mind, it was also true that at that time there were very few orchestras in the country with the capability of performing them.

So both artistically and commercially, Elgar was frustrated and the feeling grew within him that his career was heading in completely the wrong direction.

Ironically, this was made all the worse when towards the end of the decade he received by far his most important commission by that time – to write the major choral work – known as a 'Cantata' - for the Leeds Festival of 1898.

This was one of the most important festivals in the UK at that time, attracting some of the greatest names in European music. Its chief conductor was no less than the great Sir Arthur Sullivan, one of the foremost classical composers of the era and world famous through his collaboration with William Gilbert in the Savoy Operettas – works like 'The Mikado', 'Iolanthe' and 'The Gondoliers' which are still highly popular today.

Elgar had tried to persuade the festival authorities to accept something which he wished to write – he commented in a letter to his publishers that he had *'hinted at other things'* but the Festival Committee had insisted on a Cantata.

Elgar really had little choice in the matter – his reputation was growing, and the Leeds Festival would certainly enhance that. He had been offered the most important element in the whole Festival week after all. Also he needed the money from the Festival Commission and the publishing rights.

So doubtless with a degree of reluctance, he accepted the commission and set about producing a work based on the legend of the Iron Age British King Caractacus, who, according to folk law, stood defiant against the invading Roman Army until he was betrayed and captured – at the Malvern Hills, near to where Elgar was living at the time.

He conceived it as a dramatic, almost operatic piece, at a time when he was heavily influenced by the operas of Wagner.

The importance of the commission was not lost on him. If successful, it might elevate him in the musical world – but if he failed, his career might easily decline, and he would be written off as yet another composer who may have produced one or two works of merit, but when the big opportunity arose, he had proved unworthy.

As a result he was most uneasy throughout its composition and on the very day he finished it, he poured out his feelings in a letter to a friend:

'I have today written the last note on the score of 'Caractacus' & feel free. I am bursting to talk to you but when I come to hold the pen it seems to want to write 'Please be lenient': I feel frightened at my score (which is big) & if I ask for justice, surely I shall hang?'

In the event, the performance was a success with Elgar receiving rapturous applause from the audience and press reports hailing a bold new work. But it appears it did little to lighten his mood.

During his time in Leeds, he rubbed shoulders with other composers whose works were also performed at the Festival. These included the British composers Charles Villiers Stanford, and Sir Hubert Parry as well as those from abroad including the German composer of the popular opera 'Hansel and Gretel' Englebert

Humperdinck and the French composer Gabriel Fauré. He also had two personal meetings with Sullivan, who invited him and his wife to attend the Savoy Theatre for performances of two of his operettas. This they did in a 10 day visit to London immediately after the festival in which they toured various concert venues, including the Crystal Palace where excerpts from 'Caractacus' were performed.

After that, they returned to their home in Malvern – and Elgar went back to his life as a provincial music teacher.

The contrast between such a return and the glittering success of the week in Leeds where he was greeted as an equal by some of the leading musical names of the era – and then touring London venues hearing his newly composed music, must have struck home, and could easily have contributed to his gloomy mood.

One week he had stood as an equal to some of the most successful composers of the time – the following week he was back to being a provincial violin teacher again.

One of the regular teaching sessions he had in those days was at The Mount, the boarding school for the daughters of genteel families owned and operated by his friend and subsequent biographer Rosa Burley. He spent a day per week teaching the girls there and it appears the relationship he had with them could be summed up in the sentence: *'They detested him and he in turn detested them'*. As Rosa wrote in her memoir some years later:

'From various sources I learned that he was not always good-tempered and that in consequence the girls were afraid of him. Thus it was the custom for each pupil at the end of her lesson to telegraph the state of the emotional atmosphere to her successor and there was one child who enraged him to such an extent that the others had begged that she might be placed last on the list in order to prevent her from making things impossible for them.'

After one of these sessions, in October 1898, shortly after he had returned from his London holiday which had followed the Leeds Festival he made his weary way back home and in the evening, so the story goes, he sat at the piano and started playing music as it came into his head. Suddenly, his wife, Alice who was apparently sitting in the room said something like : *'That's a good tune'*, and Elgar who was relaxing as he played and enjoying a good cigar woke up from his reverie not knowing what she was talking about. After a little discussion, he tried to retrieve what he had been playing and after a few minutes Alice identified the tune again, asking what it was. He apparently replied that he did not know *'but something might be made of it.'*

During the course of the evening, they played a little parlour game together, with Elgar playing the tune in different manners to reflect the characters of people that they knew and asking Alice if she could identify each person as he played.

That was the birth of the *'Variations'* idea.

A set of 'Variations' is a musical work where a composer takes a tune – it can be any tune by anyone; it doesn't have to be necessarily an original tune by the composer – and the tune is played in various different ways. It can be played slowly, fast and in different keys and rhythms and can be embellished with further musical elements. In this way, the tune appears in different guises, but is still recognisable throughout. There are many examples of such works in the classical repertoire. Beethoven wrote a set called the *'Diabelli Variations'*, Brahms wrote the *'St Anthony Variations'*, and in more modern times Rachmaninov wrote *'Rhapsody on a Theme of Paganini'* which is also a set of variations. But Elgar's *'Enigma' Variations* remain one of the best known of them all.

What sets Elgar's work apart is the fact that in that evening parlour game with his wife, he hit upon the idea of making each different *'variation'* into a character portrait of a set of people which he and his wife knew – summed up in the dedication of the work *'To My Friends Pictured Within'*.

The idea possessed him and almost immediately, as the notion was in his head he wrote enthusiastically to his friend and mentor August Jaeger, his Editor at his publishers, Novellos:

'I have sketched a set of Variations (orkestry) on an original theme...the Variations have amused me because

I've labelled 'em with the nicknames of my particular friends...that is to say I've written the variations each one to represent the mood of the 'party' – I've liked to imagine the 'party' writing the var: him (or her) self & have written what I think they wd have written – if they were asses enough to compose – it's a quaint idee & the result is amusing to those behind the scenes & won't affect the hearer who 'nose nuffin'. What do you think ?'

But the response was lukewarm to say the least.

Elgar had proposed a complicated work for a very large orchestra that was not only expensive to publish, but which was unlikely to be performed that often – given the fact that in those days there were not that many orchestras competent enough to perform it. In fact the piece had still to be performed in the Bristol area more than 25 years after it was composed.

So the whole project was put on the back burner, despite the odd remark in Elgar's letters to the publishers saying that he had not given up on the project, that he thought it was good and so on and so forth.

Novellos, for their part it seems, had tried to persuade him to write short, easy pieces, such as the popular *'Henry VIII Dances'* composed by his contemporary, and master of the light classical genre, Edward German. The suggestions were rejected.

Elgar put his feelings about this in a letter to Jaeger:

'No – I'm not happy at all in fact never was more miserable in my life: I don't see that I've done any good at all: if I write a tune you all say it's commonplace – if I don't, you all say it's rot – well I've written Caractacus, earning thro' it 15s a week [about £60 in today's money] *while doing it & that's all – NOW if I will write any easy, small choral-society work for Birmingham, using the Festival as an advert – your firm will be 'disposed to consider it' – but my own natural bent I must choke off. No thank you – no more music for me – at present… 'Gordon' symphony. I like this idee but my dear man WHY should I try ? I can't see – I have to earn money somehow & it is NO GOOD trying this sort of thing even for a 'living wage' & your firm wouldn't give £5 for it - I tell you I am sick of it all: why can't I be encouraged to do decent stuff & not hounded into triviality…'*

Despite his mood, the publishers' lack of interest in what he wanted to write, and their suggestions as to what they wanted instead, he pressed ahead with the *Variations* and eventually completed them.

There seemed little point in sending them straight to Novellos but following advice, the finished manuscript was sent to the London based concert agent for one of the greatest conductors in the world at that time, the Austrian-Hungarian Hans Richter.

When he had a chance to study the music, Richter not only liked it, but made arrangements to perform it at a series of headline concerts he was to give in London the following June.

Novellos, for their part, then agreed to publish the *Variations* – but the level of their enthusiasm may be judged from the fact that they offered Elgar for the copyright, just one guinea (about £80 in today's money).

Elgar's mood at completing the whole thing can be indicated from the Italian inscription he wrote at the end of the manuscript –'*Bramo assai, poco spero, nulla chieggio*'. It translates to *'I crave for much, I have little hope, and I have asked for nothing.'*

So once again, Elgar had produced a masterpiece, but received scant financial reward for his efforts.

In despair he wrote to his friend Jaeger: '...*for the last six weeks (about) I have been very sick at heart over music – the whole future seems so hopeless… Now I have worked steadily and honestly till I am offered all the festivals & then the firm seem to have had enough of me.'*

'I can quite understand that my big works don't pay -i.e. show any good return but I shd. have hoped that on artistic grounds the very small remuneration I ask shd. be forthcoming for things which at least interest the better portion of the musical public. No! The only suggestion made is that the Henry VIII dances are the

thing – now I can't write that sort of thing & my own heartfelt ideas are not wanted.

'You see I want so little: £300 [about £25,000 today] *a year I must make, and that's all. Last year I subsisted on £200* [about £16,000 today]. *It seems strange that a man who might do good work shd be absolutely stopped - but that's what it means.*

'*Now you see how things are, do not tell anyone all this or any of it. I did not intend to write as it may seem disloyal to the firm but apparently this is the end of all things, so it doesn't matter.*'

And to another friend he wrote this: '*I have denied myself almost every pleasure - even a solitary cigar - & have subsisted on less wages than the merest clerk for three years & now although my 'things' are going on - more than anyone else's just now - my labour is in vain & the publishers only want me to use my position to advertise & sell - well, rot!*'

In the event, the *Variations* were a stunning success and have rightly taken their place at the forefront of popular classical music.

However, there are three aspects to the work which have set it apart from everything else that Elgar wrote in his career, and have caused almost monumental debate ever since.

The first is the novelty of each *Variation* representing someone who Elgar knew at the time – each piece identified either by a person's initials or a nickname. The completed work features 14 such 'portraits' – with Elgar's wife, Alice, representing the first and Elgar himself representing the last, and the rest, largely made up of musical portraits of people they knew in Malvern and surrounding areas.

It was an intriguing notion, but not unique. Schumann, for example, had produced such a work called *'Carnival'* in which the personalities of his wife, Chopin, Paganini and of Schumann himself in different moods are reflected by the various movements.

There was also a work by the English composer Cipriani Potter called *'The Enigma Variations and Fantasia, on a favourite Irish Air, for the Pianoforte, in the style of Five Eminent Artists, composed and dedicated to the Originals'* which had appeared in 1825 and was also based on the idea of depicting people in its various musical movements – in this case leading musicians of the time including Rossini and possibly Beethoven.

Elgar made a deliberate reference to the *'friends pictures within'* to whom the work is dedicated in the programme notes on the first performance – even though his actual note went like this:

'Mr Elgar's variations are intended to be listened to simply as absolute music. The composer himself expressly said: 'It is true that I have sketched for their amusement and mine, the idiosyncrasies of fourteen of my friends, not necessarily musicians; but this is a

personal matter and need not have been mentioned publicly.'

There were two exceptions as far as the location of the 'friends' was concerned. The first was August Jaeger himself – immortalised as 'Nimrod', a name referring to the translation of Jaeger's German surname, which in English means 'Hunter', and thus the allusion to the fabled hunter of ancient literature.

The second was the variation listed at number 13 in the cycle.

This is the subject of the next chapter in this book – and is the second aspect which sets this work apart and which has set scholars writing volumes ever since - because whoever this person was, their identity was never revealed. Elgar took it with him to the grave, and only indicated it with three asterisks, together with the subtitle *'Romanza'* – i.e. *'Romance'*.

And of course, with such a title to the piece, there has been considerable speculation, not only as to who this person was, but also what sort of a relationship did they have with the composer. But more of that in the next chapter.

But the third aspect which makes this such a talked about and intriguing work is the very title of the piece itself and a mysterious reference which Elgar allowed to be placed in the programme notes on that first, fateful, performance.

Above the music the word *'Enigma'* appears, and in those programme notes, the following was written:

'The Variations should stand simple as a piece of music. The Enigma I will not explain – its dark saying must be left unguessed and I warn you that the apparent connection between the variations and the theme is often of the slightest texture; further, through and over the whole set another and larger theme goes but is not played.'

At the time, Elgar must surely have regretted allowing both of these aspects to be put into the programme notes, because almost universally, he was crucified by the critics for it.

The Guardian, for example commenting on the *'friends'* said this: *'It may indeed be regretted that the composer should have attempted to describe in his fourteen variations the personal characteristics of several intimate friends who are represented in the score by initials or sobriquets, and being unknown to the majority of the audience do not add much to the interest of the music.'*

And the Musical News chirped: *'Why distract public attention from the work itself by saying "I meant something by all this: but you cannot follow my meaning as you do not know my friends."*

And as far as the mysteries over the *'dark saying'*, were concerned, the reaction was brutal. One of the critics wrote this: *'Mr Elgar rather upset my temper by allowing some nonsense about his clever work to be printed in the programme. He warned us that the dark saying of his enigma, or theme, must be left unguessed by us and that the apparent connection between the variations and the theme is often of the slightest texture. He added – in order to confuse us all as much as possible – that the principal 'theme never appears, even as in some late dramas – the chief character is never on the stage'.*

'Mercy on us! What foolish words be these! A theme and variations and the composer tells us that the theme "must be left unguessed", and that "through and over the whole set another and larger theme 'goes' but is not played"!

'This sort of would-be profound and quite unutterable twaddle sets all sensible people against the composer who gives vent to it and against his music. It bemuses the mind.'

Elgar never revealed the solution, and neither did he, at the time, reveal the identities of the people he had portrayed. He left that vacant for 25 years, only revealing clues to the identities in notes he wrote in 1924 – and even then, did not reveal the identity of the anonymous person, represented only by three asterisks on the suitably placed 13th variation.

And yet the mystery over the 'dark saying' which he created in 1899 has resonated ever since – with 'solutions' understandably being put forward on a regular basis. After all, everyone does like a good mystery.

In the main, these 'solutions' tend to fall into two distinct camps.

There are those who feel that the key to the mystery is musical – in other words the reference which Elgar made to *'another and larger theme'* is a *musical* theme. As a result there have been many pieces of music which have been suggested, with musicologists delving deep into whatever evidence might exist to fit the music that they put forward.

A strong contender over the years has been music from Mozart's *'Prague' Symphony* which it is claimed was particularly prominent in Elgar's mind at the time, and which, coincidentally was also played on the same programme as the Variations when the work was first performed.

Another has been the popular ballad *'Auld Lang Syne'*, reflecting the idea of friendship – though Elgar specifically said that this *'will not do'* when it was suggested to him.

But over the years there have been many ideas put forward – each of which have had their champions, but equally have attracted their detractors.

The second group of solution hunters are the non-musical people – i.e. people who have sought a solution based on a hypothesis which has nothing particularly to do with music.

Many of these *'solutions'* have centred on the fact that it is known that Elgar did have an interest in riddles and cyphers. He appears to have had the sort of mind which enjoyed plays on words, and mathematical codes.

So many of the solution seekers have tried to find evidence of codes and cyphers in the music – with some producing explanations that run to almost encyclopaedic length.

Unfortunately, in recent times, as Elgar's music has begun to regain world-wide appreciation, the *'Enigma'* mystery has attracted the attention of that particularly modern fraternity, the *'conspiracy theorists'*, the type of people who decide what the solution is first and then attract all the so-called *'evidence'* to justify it, regardless of whether that *'evidence'* actually exists.

The main problem that all these solutions – whether musical, non-musical or plain ridiculous – is that Elgar never provided the definitive solution himself, and whatever is the real truth about the whole thing, it went with him to the grave.

So in effect, it is left to a matter of belief – and will remain so unless someone produces an unequivocally authentic manuscript in Elgar's hand in which he finally provides the solution from beyond the grave. Given the enormous scholarly interest over the years in every scrap of manuscript and letter which Elgar actually wrote in his life time, that prospect remains remote, as the chance of discovery of such an artefact appears virtually non-existent.

However, as with all commentators on Elgar, I suppose it is incumbent on me to provide at least what I, personally *believe* to be a suitable solution – though having said that, I must stress that this is a matter which provides *me* with an answer, and I fully accept that someone else might be just as dismissive as I have been over other 'solutions'.

I actually have two which, to me, seem plausible.

The first is that there was no mystery at all. In other words, the whole thing was fabricated by Elgar as a kind of *'PR'* stunt to promote the work.

My reasons for suggesting this are two-fold.

In the first instance, the time when the Variations emerged was an era when the public were very much interested in mysteries. Popular fiction was awash with classics of the mystery and sci-fi genres. Only a few years before H G Wells had published *'The War of the Worlds'* and *'The Time Machine'*. Bram Stoker's *'Dracula'* was published in the same year as the *Variations*, and magazines were full of gentleman sleuths such as Sherlock Holmes solving ever more impossible mysteries and crimes.

In the second instance, there was Elgar's innate ability to promote himself and his works. The fact remains that he was clearly desperate to achieve success with the *Variations,* and he did have a track record as a competent PR man writing press releases and articles to increase public awareness of his activities from even his earliest days. He also latched on to public moods by dedicating some of his works to events at the time. *'Caractacus'* for example emerged as the country was celebrating Queen Victoria's Diamond Jubilee – so he dedicated it to the Queen.

It is quite possible therefore that in order to provide an extra dimension of interest in the work, he invented the mystery.

If this was indeed the case then it may have proved totally embarrassing at the time – given the vicious reaction of the press. But then it is supremely ironic that the whole *'Enigma'* mystery has been such an enormous long-term success and has boosted the popularity of the work immensely ever since.

To me, this seems *plausible* – and in view of the press reaction at the time renders both the various musical and non-musical other solutions somewhat *implausible*.

After all, if the solution were a clever counterpoint or re-working of some other musical piece, or a remarkable cryptic cypher as has been suggested, *why* didn't Elgar provide the solution there and then ?

In June 1899 he faced fierce attacks from the press, the very people he relied upon to make his work a success, baffled by a mystery they could not unravel. Had the solution been as clever either musically or otherwise as the theorists have since put forward, it would surely be logical for him to have faced down the criticism by providing the solution.

And such a move, were it as clever and complicated as has been suggested, would surely have earned him further applause from the critics.

But he didn't.

And as a result I have long wondered whether he didn't because either he couldn't – in the sense that, as stated above, there *was* no solution and that it was just a badly thought out PR exercise which backfired – or that the real solution was something which by its very nature *had* to remain secret.

Which brings me on to the second idea which I consider *plausible* – and that is that the *'dark saying'* was inextricably linked to the people portrayed in the *Variations*.

There was no reason for Elgar to mention either matter in his programme notes. Doing so invited the ire of the press, as he was to find out – yet despite his own adamant remark that the piece was to be considered purely as *'absolute music'* and this was a stance he had taken from his original announcement of the project before he had even put it together – he still went ahead and made a major issue of it.

It would seem plausible to me therefore that the *'dark saying'*, if it existed at all, should be taken within the context of the characters portrayed.

If this is the case then it is surely an important factor as to *who* is actually represented in the work. Elgar famously dedicated it to '*my* friends pictured within', but almost without exception the people are those whose acquaintance he made only after he married his wife Alice.

There are none of the friends who had made up his circle from the days before his marriage – there was no Hugh Blair, for example, the Worcester Cathedral Organist and a long-time friend who had been instrumental in securing his first important commission, the *'Froissart'* overture for the 1890 Worcester Festival. There were none of the people with whom Elgar had played in ensembles and orchestras as a young man.

Instead, there were people like William Meath Baker, country squire and lifelong friend of Alice. He was associated with other 'Variations' – such as R B Townsend, an Oxford Don who was also his brother in law. Then there was Dora Penny, immortalised as *'Dorabella'* in the Variations, who was the step-daughter of his sister, Minnie, who also had been one of Alice's childhood friends. Three other *'Variations'* were also associated with Baker, being his close friends of his University days and several others were part of an upper middle class society into which Elgar had been introduced when he married Alice in 1889.

And then, when you examine the nature of the *'idiosyncrasies'* explored by the Variations themselves, you cannot escape the fact that they are crafted with devilish humour – to the extent that they might be today considered to be *satirical*.

Baker himself, for example, is portrayed as a pariah who issues his daily orders then strides out of the room slamming the door behind him. Townsend, the high academic and golf expert is portrayed making a fool of himself in amateur dramatics. Isobel Fitton, said to be a very competent viola player, is portrayed playing only three notes; Troyte Griffith, a Malvern architect, is shown to be useless at playing the piano. But perhaps the most satirical and some might say vicious portrait of all is reserved for Dora Penny who's speech impediment is laid out for all to hear. Apparently she had a stammer.

Another odd aspect of the work is that there is only one professional musician in the set - George Robertson Sinclair, the Organist at Hereford Cathedral. Yet it is not *he* who is portrayed but his *bulldog* Dan.

When Elgar was first introduced into such a set of upper crust people as is represented by the Variations, it must have been awkward for him. He was, after all, from a different class background at a time in society when class standing mattered.

It is quite easy to speculate that many of the friends Alice had grown up with and who were portrayed in the *Variations* must have had severe misgivings about her marrying someone they would have seen as a penniless musician who, in their view could potentially have been some sort of *'gold digger'*, and while we have no evidence to suggest either way, it is reasonable to suggest that initial meetings must have been, to say the least, awkward on both sides. Some may even have remembered him visiting their opulent homes via the tradesman's entrance in order to tune their pianos, or given violin lessons to them and their children.

Elgar carried resentments surrounding his social position and his religious background with him throughout his life and it is quite possible that these might have emerged in his music.

Certainly the background to each *Variation* portrait would seem to suggest that he was hardly providing a loving and positive view of the person portrayed, and that is perhaps why he did not reveal the identities until 25 years later, when several of them were already dead.

Over the years as I have contemplated this hypothesis, the one *Variation* character that troubled me was Winifred Norbury, who seemed to have had much milder treatment. Nothing seemed to have reflected in any satirical sense on her character. But then I read Elgar's notes and he made it clear that the *Variation* was not specifically about *her* at all. He had written: '*Really suggested by an eighteenth-century house. The gracious personalities of the ladies are sedately shown. W.N. was more connected with music than others of the family and her initials head the movement.*'

The two Variations that we can assume were definitely *not* of this particular social set were the mysterious *13th Variation*, which remained anonymous and was only indicated by three asterisks and the subtitle *'Romanza'*, and the ever popular *'Nimrod'* – nickname for August Jaeger, Elgar's Editor at his publishers.

Of the former, all that Elgar would say in his notes was that this was '*a lady who, at the time of the composition was on a sea voyage*'.

As to *'Nimrod'*, who's variation is so universally known and which is played so nobly as a stand-alone piece, it can be argued that he was placed in the *Variations* because of his professional association with the composer. He was, after all, the person who had great sway as to publication of Elgar's music.

There may, however, be a further factor which induced Elgar to include him, and also give him 'the best tune' – an observation made to Elgar by Dora Penny when she asked him why he had done so.

The fact remained that Jaeger, like Elgar, was hardly of the upper middle class social standing of the rest.

Perhaps their view of him could be summed up in a passage from Rosa Burley's reminiscence : *'He was a lovable but rather typically commonplace little German with a very large head and a guttural accent and it was apparent from the outset that he was not only deeply impressed with Edward's ability but inclined to worship him as a hero.'*

His inclusion, and the fact that he had *'the best tune'* may therefore have been a slight slap in the face of the others – though it is also true that Jaeger was Elgar's Editor at his publishers and therefore his inclusion may have been in the mould of a *'homage to the boss'*. Certainly, when Elgar first proposed the idea of the work, in his initial letter written to Jaeger, he made it quite clear that he would be the centrepiece – *'you are Nimrod'*, he wrote.

But perhaps the final suggestion that this work celebrated *'friends'* who had much more to do with Alice rather than Elgar himself was his own *Variation*, which he identified as *'EDU'* rather than *'E.E.'* – *'Edu'* being the nickname which Alice had for him rather than his own identity. So perhaps he was even identifying himself also as one of *her* friends.

As I have said, until a definitive solution written undeniably in Elgar's hand emerges, we shall never know. And, given the ingenious mastery of the writing of the work is can be deemed irrelevant anyway – the *'Enigma Variations'* stands as one of the great masterpieces of British music in its own right, regardless of any mystery about its composition.

The only other point I would add is that any clever interpretation of either music or cryptography does not appear to be an element in any other of his works – there is no publicly stated *'enigma'* or *'dark saying'* attached to his two symphonies, to any of his choral works, *Pomp & Circumstance Marches,* overtures, or, it appears, anything else he produced.

Perhaps the vicious reaction of the press encouraged him to desist, or perhaps he had vented his spleen sufficiently. Who knows ?

The *'solution hunters'* will never go away, I am sure, and there will be many more propositions put forward, some as mere suggestions, some as *'definitive'* according to the nature and ego of the proposer. It's simply a matter of your own personal taste.

THE MYSTERY OF THE THIRTEENTH VARIATION

One of the most intriguing mysteries surrounding Elgar's music concerns the identity of the inspiration of the Thirteenth Variation of the *'Enigma Variations'*.

As I discussed in the previous chapter, the work itself is surrounded by mysteries concerning its original theme, and the programme notes which Elgar allowed to be printed for the first performance.

But there remains a further mystery concerning the thirteen variation, which itself has intrigued scholars and theorists ever since it first appeared.

The fact remains that while the rest of the variations, which Elgar clearly said were portraits of people he and his wife knew at the time, he left the identity of the inspiration of the thirteenth deliberately anonymous.

Whereas clues were left as to the identities of the rest of the variations – through either initials or nicknames printed above each piece on the score, that of the thirteenth was left as merely three asterisks, with the further tantalising addition of *'Romanza'* underneath.

In 1924, some 25 years after the work was written, Elgar was asked to write notes for a set of pianola rolls which were issued for the work, and he duly supplied sufficient information to allow the identification of each of the characters portrayed.

Even then it surprised people. As the leading music critic, Robin Legge wrote in his Daily Telegraph article about the work : *'We know or thought we did, each variation apart from its purely musical interest, to be very much a musical portrait of somebody known to the composer. It is not too much to say that after reading what Sir Edward tells us on these rolls, every writer on Elgar, every annotator of the "Enigma" variations, will need to revise what he has written.'*

However, the identity of the person behind the thirteenth variation was once again left anonymous. All that Elgar would say in his notes was : *'The asterisks take the place of the name of a lady who was, at the time of the composition, on a sea voyage.'*

In this regard, the music itself is somewhat mysterious, with a section in which Elgar instructs the timpani drummer to place a coin on his drums, so that the sound is like the rumblings of a ship's engines, and over it, the rest of the orchestra play a directly quoted passage from Mendelssohn's Overture *'A Calm Sea and Prosperous Voyage'* – perhaps the only time a composer has made such a direct quotation – complete with quotation marks in the score – in the history of music. Elgar certainly wished to make his musical point !

As with so many Elgarian mysteries, the fact that such a piece combined intrigue with the concealed identity of a woman – especially with the added indication of *'Romanza'*, has led to widespread speculation.

It has to be said, however, that as Elgar also took this mystery to his grave, then any conclusive solution must remain no more than speculation. There are, however, some candidates and it worth discussing each of their claims.

An official identity has for many years been given to Lady Mary Lygon, of Madresfield Court, near Malvern – a place, incidentally which was the inspiration for Evelyn Waugh's modern classic 'Brideshead Revisited'.

She was a long standing friend of the Elgars and heavily involved in the musical activities in the Worcestershire area, founding a local musical competition in which Elgar took part. He also dedicated his early work *'Three Characteristic Pieces'* to her.

The reason why she was originally identified as the inspiration for the variation was that it is known she had undertaken a long sea voyage to visit her brother who was a leading colonial civil servant in Australia. Later research unearthed an early sketch of the variation in Elgar's hand marked 'LML' – and this was assumed to stand for 'Lady Mary Lygon'.

For many years this seemed to suffice – particularly as there was absolutely no suggestion that anything more than an intimate friendship existed between Elgar and Lady Mary – who was no less than one of Queen Victoria's Ladies in Waiting, and the sister of an Earl – and therefore hardly the subject of any suggestions of impropriety.

However in more recent times, her claim has been questioned – mainly because the long sea voyage she undertook was some years *after* the *Variations* had been written, and in fact the very day the piece was finally completed, she was actually sitting having tea with Elgar's wife, Alice, at their Malvern home.

It follows that if Elgar's declared specification that the lady in question was on a sea voyage *'at the time of the composition'* then it could not be her.

The assumption that the 'LML' on the sketch referred to her has also been called into question mainly because if it was to work then the first initial 'L' had to mean 'Lady' – and none of the other variations carry such titles in their initials.

For the past few decades, attention has been turned to a shadowy figure who is now thought to be Elgar's first love.

Her name was Helen Weaver, the daughter of the owner of the shoe shop near the Elgar family music business in High Street, Worcester. Her brother, Frank, was a violinist who played with Elgar in orchestras in the area.

Helen, a talented musician herself, was fortunate enough to study at the Leipzig Academy and it is claimed that Elgar not only fell deeply in love with her but also proposed marriage.

The passage of love, however, rarely runs smoothly, and it is claimed in some versions of the story that Helen broke off the engagement and went to live in New Zealand, apparently because she was suffering from some sort of respiratory condition which required fresh air for her recovery. In some accounts this illness is given to TB, in others it was a consequence of smallpox.

An early love affair, even one which apparently was planned to lead to marriage but which eventually fell by the wayside would hardly be considered worthy of much study, but in this case it's claimed Elgar was so devastated by this episode that he carried the pain of their separation with him for the rest of his life, and furthermore Helen's ghost haunts much of his later music and *she* is the mysterious inspiration of the thirteenth variation.

Addressing the mystery, the leading music critic Ernest Newman, wrote the following to an enquirer in 1943:

'There's no doubt any longer about the meaning of the "Enigma". I have the name, but cannot publish it. An old lady who had known Elgar in his youth wrote me and told me the whole curious story and gave me the name, but under the pledge of secrecy.

'It was a girl he was in love with, and she in love with him; but the difference in their faiths was a bar to marriage. She went to Australia or New Zealand – I forget which at this moment – and died there.

'It was <u>this</u> voyage that Elgar was commemorating in one of the Enigma Variations.

Another source of information is provided by Wulstan Atkins, son of the Worcester Cathedral Organist, and Elgar's lifelong friend, Sir Ivor Atkins.

In his book, *'The Elgar Atkins Friendship'* published in 1984, he makes similar statements to Newman – but this time based on a conversation which his father apparently had with Elgar in 1932.

Wulstan Atkins was not present at the meeting himself, and his father only told him about it some years after Elgar's death.

He then continues*: 'He said that he was in a difficult position. Elgar had not stipulated that the matter was confidential, but for nearly fifty years he had never disclosed his first engagement and my father was certain that Carice* [Elgar's daughter] *did not know about it.*

'On the other hand he felt that this experience had profoundly affected much of Elgar's music and should, therefore, at some time be revealed. After much thought my father considered that in order to avoid any possible distress it should be kept secret until fifty years after Elgar's death, and hence his disclosure to me on the understanding that I would ensure that this information became known in 1984.'

Atkins then states that Elgar had arrived in Leipzig on New Year's Day 1883, and stayed for two weeks and during that time *'fell deeply in love with Helen, who returned his love'*.

'They agreed to meet again in Worcester on her return at the end of the Leipzig term and they became engaged. Their families however stipulated that no engagement should be announced until Helen had finished the remaining two years at Leipzig and the difference in their religions could be resolved. Many letters were exchanged during Helen's stay in Leipzig.'

Following Helen's return, things did not run smoothly with the romance and *'in June or July 1884 they agreed to break off their engagement, mainly, my father gathered, because of their different religions and as was the custom in those days, agreed to return each other's letters. Miss Weaver went away to teach and to stay with her friend Edith in Bradford. At some stage she contracted smallpox which left her with distressing asthma.*

'In the autumn of 1885 Helen Weaver decided to go to New Zealand and later died there.'

The story is certainly seductive.

Who would not wish to believe such a romantic story of love lost ? A musical genius, deemed 'penniless' in some accounts, falling in love with a beautiful young girl, enjoying a romance through a long hot summer of their youth and he proposes marriage. They become engaged, but she rejects him, because of the differences in their religion, and she departs to live out her life on the other side of the world leaving him bereft and emotionally scarred for life – so much so that the ghost of his lost love haunts some of his greatest work.

But where is the firm evidence to support this ?

The only contemporaneous references seem to be in letters he wrote to his friend Dr Charles Buck, a Yorkshire Doctor who Elgar befriended in his early 20s. But the references are remarkably brief.

'The vacation at Leipzig begins shortly, my "Braut" [German for 'Bride'] *arrives here on Thursday next; remaining 'till the first week in Septr: of course I shall remain in Worcester 'till her departure.'* [1 July 1883]

'Well Helen has come back! Mrs Weaver [her mother] *is so ill, dying in fact, so the child thought it best to return and nurse her so we are together a little now and then and consequently happy.'* [11 November 1883]

'P.S Miss Weaver is remaining in Worcester and the little music &c that we get together is the only enjoyment I get and more than I deserve no doubt.' [14 January 1884]

'My prospects are about as hopeless as ever ...Miss Weaver is very well. I do not think that she will remain in Worcester much longer now.' [21 April 1884]

'I will not worry you with my particulars but must tell you that things have not prospered with me this year at all, my prospects are worse than ever & to crown my

miseries my engagement is broken off & I am lonely.'
[20 July 1884]

'...of course all these things are of no account, but they serve to divert me somewhat & hide a broken heart.' [8 March 1885]

'Miss W is going to New Zealand this month – her lungs are affected I hear & there has been a miserable time for me since I came home.' [7 October 1885].

There can be little doubt from these references that there had been some sort of a romance between Elgar and Helen at that time, but was it strong enough to have affected the rest of Elgar's creative life ?

The references are fleeting and from the chronology of the letters the relationship does not appear to have lasted too long. Six months separate *'Braut'* and *'Miss W'*. Furthermore, the reference to *'Braut'* is deliberately put into quotation marks, as though it might be taken as a *'term'* which might only indicate an aspiration of Elgar's part.

If she was to be his bride – at a time when proposal to marry was taken most seriously as a form of contract – there also seems to be a remarkable lack of announcement of it in his letters.

Elgar corresponded frequently with Buck at this time – indeed his letters provide some of the only insights into his life during this period. Many of the letters were extensive and it is clear that Buck was the sort of friend with whom Elgar could discuss personal matters.

Yet the only reference to any engagement to be married – surely a somewhat important matter to discuss with such a friend – appears to be that which announced that the whole affair had come to an end. There may have been other letters, long lost, of course, and we will never know what verbal conversations took place between the two young men, but this is the only evidence which remains, and even here, Elgar refers to the breaking off of the engagement as an added tribulation to other traumas of his life – mainly financial it seems - at that time. It does not appear to be the central devastating event which had overtaken him.

So was this a formal engagement – or some fanciful idea of Elgar's part?

After the 'engagement' came to an end, there is no evidence that Elgar attempted to win her back nor prevent her leaving England. There appears to be no surviving correspondence between them, either before, during or after the *'engagement'* and it would seem that none has come to light, despite the fact that in his book, Wulstan Atkins states that there were many letters. His explanation, as relayed to him by his father that after the *'engagement'* had ended, Elgar and Helen gave the letters back to each other might explain the lack of any correspondence relating directly to any marriage proposal. If there were a considerable number of letters, then presumably they were destroyed by both parties, otherwise they would surely have long appeared by now. But it is certainly the case that, despite the fact that there has been considerable publication of Elgar's letters in many volumes, not one single letter to or from Helen seems to have survived and this is surely somewhat strange considering how close they must have been for a friendship and subsequently a love affair with intention to lead on to marriage to develop.

Another question arises as to the length of time the relationship lasted. Helen was, according to all accounts, pursuing her studies in Leipzig. Elgar travelled there for just two weeks. She came back for a period and again they were together, but only for a matter of weeks before she returned to Leipzig, and after that it appears the relationship came to an end.

While it is doubtless the case that they knew each other well because of living so close in Worcester and Elgar's friendship with Helen's brother, the period of their relationship nevertheless appears short and patchy.

Elgar was in his mid-20s when these events occurred. Helen was younger by four or five years. Young people harbour many romantic feelings, but the bald reality of life is that many a relationship at that age founders on the rocks, with the inevitable emotional traumas, the bitterness and recrimination which can ensue.

Most of us in our lifetimes have experienced similar episodes, and may, in later life reflect in our private moments on *'what might have been'*. But did any past relationship loom so large in the memory as a matter of such profound regret to have affected us for the rest of our lives ?

There is no reason to doubt that Elgar was enamoured sufficiently to have proposed marriage, and it was natural that he should be devastated when, subsequently the relationship not only broke down, but Helen also travelled to the other side of the world, never to return.

But does this necessarily mean that he was so devastated by all this that he was still reeling from its effects many years later, and as a result wove memories of lost love into some of his finest works, written many years later at the height of his maturity as a composer?

One further piece of evidence of what took place, was a personal reminiscence of a friend of Helen's who was with her in Leipzig at the time. She speaks of Elgar and the various activities in which the three of them were involved – but there is no mention of any marriage proposal, nor indeed, that Elgar and Helen were deeply in love. Her reminiscence speaks of good times, enjoyed by all.

Once again, however, this account must be considered anecdotal as it was written as a letter to Elgar's daughter, Carice, many years after the events, and of course references to Elgar's romance may have been deliberately removed from the account in deference to Carice.

In the years that followed the collapse of his *'engagement'* Elgar doubtless had other relationships. Another letter to Buck only a few months after the *'engagement'* ended makes reference to someone called 'Miss E.E. at Inverness', who is dismissed as *' nobody – that is to say that I shall ever see her again. I wrote down the little air when I was there and dedicated to her "with estimation the most profound", as a Frenchman would say, that's all.'*

So it seems even a short time after the engagement ended Elgar had been involved in another liaison.

Most of Elgar's relationships from this period of his life remain unknown – there are simply no references in any correspondence. But there were at least two that we do know of.

The first was Gertrude Walker, daughter of a country Squire who was also a curate in Worcestershire. Elgar was again said to have proposed marriage, but when her father found out he put a stop to it.

Unlike Helen Weaver, however, Gertrude remained in contact with Elgar, and they remained friends for the rest of their lives. He even tried to assist her career as a singer when he had achieved fame in the musical world himself.

The second relationship, with Alice Roberts, the daughter of a Major General in the Indian Army, blossomed into a marriage which lasted 30 years.

Shortly after they were married, in 1889, Elgar wrote the following to Dr Buck – the references this time are in stark contrast to what he wrote about Helen:

'I must tell you how happy I am in my new life & what a dear, loving companion I have & how sweet everything seems & how understandable existence seems to have grown…I think all the difficult problems are now solved and – well I don't worry myself about 'em now!'

It would seem difficult to equate the feelings he was expressing at this time – when he was 32 years of age – to a man secretly harbouring the feelings of true love for someone else, who had long departed his life.

To make such a suggestion would mean, by definition, that his wife of 30 years was in some way a substitute and as such his feelings for her could never have been complete – and that no matter what happiness he might have enjoyed with his wife, he was always looking back to 'what might have been'.

This is surely absurd, given that they had such a stable marriage which was only cut short when Alice died in 1920 – an event which by all contemporary accounts devastated him.

The 'evidence' as such which supports fond stories of lost love and that this girl from the past was a yearning memory written into a mysterious anonymous section of the *Enigma Variations*, hardly amounts to anything which might be considered conclusive.

Indeed, if Elgar's definition of the person portrayed, written 25 years later, is to be believed, it could *not* be her. He had stipulated that the lady in question had been on a sea voyage *at the time the Variations were written*. If this is the case then it could not be Helen, as she had travelled to New Zealand some 14 years before.

Such romantic suggestions of a devastated genius looking back in time to lost love at the time he composed the *Enigma Variations* is also hardly compatible with a general comment about women which he made, *at the time he was writing the Variations,* in a letter to his friend August Jaeger: '*... a woman's not worth a damn who won't put up with everything except ineptitude and crime.*'

It would seem, therefore, that the evidence which supports this story is hardly conclusive. It amounts to no more than a few references in letters to a friend, a testimony by an anonymous old woman recalling something from years before, expressed in a letter to Ernest Newman, and the report of a conversation many years after it had taken place, between Elgar and Ivor Atkins.

Furthermore, Atkins had apparently said that '*Elgar had not stipulated that the matter was confidential*' – which hardly allies with the matter being so heart-rending that its disclosure should remain secret.

The confidentiality seems to have been applied by Newman and Atkins, who seem to have regarded this almost in the category of a state secret, and it would seem at least plausible that weaving such secrecy around the story has given it far more weight than perhaps it really deserved.

It also appears from Wulstan Atkins' account that the extrapolation, that *'this experience had profoundly affected much of Elgar's music'* had been created by his father. There is no evidence in the Atkins account that Elgar had actually stated that as fact.

To sum up, therefore : that Elgar had a relationship with this girl seems undeniable. That he actually proposed marriage to her seems possible. That it devastated him to the extent that it haunted his subsequent creative life, given the lack of firm evidence, seems highly questionable – and thus calls into question that Helen was the subject of this *Variation*.

The 'LML' reference on the original sketch has however been speculated as being an indication of a German phrase : *'Liebling meine Liebe'* meaning 'My dear Love' -but of course this could not necessarily mean a reference to Helen.

There is, however a third candidate, but the claim relies almost entirely on a reminiscence by the great American conductor Leopold Stokowski.

The lady in question was an American socialite named Julia Worthington, who is known to have been a close friend of the Elgars from an early time – but whose relationship with Elgar has long been the subject of speculation.

She was a divorcee originally married to an American industrialist, and extremely rich in her own right. She was known to her closest friends as *'Pippa'* – but although it is indicated that there must have been considerable correspondence between both Elgar and his wife with her, hardly a single letter seems to have survived – and to this day not a single letter from Elgar *to* her appears to have come to light.

Such a lack of such evidence has led to inevitable speculation that such letters were destroyed – leading equally inevitably to speculation as to why.

The connection between her and the *'Romanza'* Variation derives from a radio broadcast Stokowski gave in 1972. The broadcast featured his reminiscences when he was a young organ student in London in the early 1900s and in it he made this reference: *"I met a girl, an American girl. We became friends. She introduced me to her sister who was a married lady and very beautiful. I used to go to the sister's house.*

'One night the door opened and in walked a man. Elgar. Now of course I didn't know him I was only a student then – but I knew his photograph. I knew his face. And gradually I began to notice that Elgar was very much in love with the sister who was a very beautiful and brilliant person and this went on and on. After a time she had to go back to America and while she was on a ship

he was composing the Enigma Variations. You will notice that one of those variations has no initials and it has a quotation from Mendelssohn...

He then went on : *'Now Elgar was, first of all a great artist and then he was a really fine personality. He was married, he was true to his wife and yet he was in love with this girl and this was a great tragedy of Elgar's life...'*

This, of course, may be merely the confused recollections of a man who by that time was in his eighties. However, Mrs Worthington *did* have a London home at that time, and she *is* known to have been particularly close to Elgar. When he was established internationally, he went to America and spent time with her and she in turn visited the Elgars in England – and the mere fact that there is such little written evidence of their actual relationship could speak volumes.

We shall never know definitively. Like the overall mysteries of the *Enigma Variations* themselves it is highly unlikely to say the least that any definitive evidence in terms of a solution written in Elgar's hand is ever going to emerge. The mysteries remain with him in the grave.

But whatever is the explanation, Elgar obviously did not wish the identity of this mystery woman to be revealed – and ever since the musical world has speculated why.

THE MYSTERY OF THE 'SOUL' OF ELGAR'S VIOLIN CONCERTO ?

Elgar's violin concerto might not be as well-known as his later cello concerto, but it is nevertheless one of his finest works. It is also one of the longest violin concertos in the repertoire, and without doubt one of the most emotional.

It dates from the height of his powers as a composer, and was first performed by Fritz Kreisler in 1910. Elgar gave the formal dedication to Kreisler, but above the music as it appeared in the printed score, he placed a strange inscription in Spanish: *'Aquí está encerrada el alma de.....'*
Romantically translated as *'Herein is enshrined the soul of .....'*, Elgar further enhanced the mystery by putting five dots at the end of the quotation in place of the universally accepted three dots to indicate a missing word.
Theories have abounded as to the meaning of this strange inscription and with the advent of the internet, just as with the *'Enigma Variations'* and it's *'dark saying'* all sorts of notions have been put forward some of them plausible, some remarkable and others quite ridiculous.

But just as with many of the other mysteries surrounding Elgar's life and works, this was another one he took to his grave, so everything is once again in the realm of conjecture and interpretation – with the *'evidence'* such as it is, remaining scant to say the least.

Of course, the missing word could be something as simple and innocent as a notion, or inanimate object which happens to have five letters – *'music'* for example, or even *'Elgar'*. In fact, one leading violinist even quipped, seeing that the quotation is in Spanish, that it could refer to *'El Gar'*.

In one of the few clues which Elgar is said to have provided himself, he apparently said that the identity was *'female'* – but this so called *'revelation'* came from a report of a third party conversation which he supposedly had with one of his earliest biographers.

But, assuming that the missing word *was* 'female' the generally accepted wisdom is that the quotation referred to a woman of Elgar's intimate acquaintance who obviously had a name which could be fitted somehow into five letters.

And following on to *that*: if the quotation *does* refer to a woman – what *exactly* was the nature of her relationship with Elgar ?

Given the romantic nature of the music – with Elgar himself admitting on one occasion that even *he* wondered if it might be *'too emotional'* it is easy to see why people have agonised for more than a century over this missing word – particularly if it referred to some sort of clandestine *'dark lady'* in his life.

So, if we accept for the sake of argument that this may indeed have been a person, and that she was female, who might this lady be ?

Over the years, speculation has put forward three candidates – though recently, a fourth has also been added.

The first, is yet again Helen Weaver, his *'braut'* from Leipzig, who allegedly broke Elgar's heart when he was 25.

The leading music critic Ernest Newman was convinced it was her, bearing in mind *'Helen'* has five letters.

When he wrote his first night critique of the concerto, he was obviously referring to this when he made this reference:

'It looks back in more ways than one to the famous 'Enigma' Variations and the Spanish words suggest that as in them, there is a personal significance in the new work.

'More than this, there is a theme which reminds us strongly of a theme in the last of the Variations and it is hard to believe that the same individual has not inspired both.'

But he cites no firm evidence to support this opinion and in all honesty it does seem implausible that this girl would be such a vital subject of a work written more than a quarter of a century after she had departed Elgar's life – bearing in mind that her spectre doesn't seem to appear in any other work he wrote either at this time, nor subsequently.

The second candidate is the one who has been suggested in more recent times – and her name was Mrs Dora Adeline Nelson.

Her identity was revealed in an article by Elgar's biographer Michael Kennedy alleging she and Elgar had been lovers and had a daughter together. Dora was nicknamed *'Peggy'* and the daughter, *'Pearl'* - both having five letters.

The alleged affair was revealed when the composer William Walton, who apparently had known about it for some time contacted Kennedy suggesting he investigate.

Kennedy discovered that in the 1940s Mrs Nelson was a cook for the art historian Sir Kenneth Clark and had asked him to sign some official papers for *'Pearl'*.

When Clark looked at the documents, he was intrigued to see that her surname was given as *'Elgar'*, and Mrs Nelson promptly told him that the girl was Elgar's love child - who apparently was born around 1905-06.

Subsequent research by others latching onto the story suggested that Mrs Nelson – just like Helen Weaver - was both the inspiration of the 13th Variation and the *'soul'* of the violin concerto.

But this claim lacks any firm evidence to substantiate it and it would seem to be nothing more than mere conjecture.

No correspondence linking Elgar with either of these two women has come to light, nor indeed any other evidence from any other third parties.

While it is quite possible that he *might* have had an affair – after all these things *do* happen – it seems implausible to say the least that this would have led to the composition of such an intensely romantic work, particularly as it was composed under the gaze of Elgar's wife.

The third candidate is **Lady Alice Stuart-Wortley**, a daughter of the Pre-Raphaelite artist Sir John Everett Millais, and wife of the Conservative MP for Sheffield Hallam.

Her claim, is considered much more plausible and attracts support from many Elgar researchers, mainly because there is much more circumstantial evidence.

Elgar had first known Alice since 1902 through their mutual friend the financier Frank Schuster, and their relationship flourished. There was a lively correspondence throughout their lives – enough to fill a 500 page book when the letters were published some years ago.

Letters written by Elgar to her refer to it as *'our own concerto',* and by the time the concerto was finished he had called her *'Windflower'* – and there are a number of themes in the concerto which he also dubbed *'Windflower'* themes.

One of the main proponents of her being the *'soul'* of the concerto is once again Michael Kennedy.

In his book, published in the 1960s he quotes from various letters Elgar wrote to her such as this:

'I have been working hard at the windflower themes – but all stands still until you come and approve.'

And again : *'The tunes stick and are not windflowerish at present.'*

Kennedy also makes reference to a letter to Frank Schuster in which he says : *'I want to end that concerto but I do not see my way very clearly to the end so you had best invite its stepmother.'*

He then concludes: *'It is impossible not to infer from these statements that hers was the soul of the work especially when one discovers on a sheet of her notepaper the Spanish quotation which heads the work in Elgar's writing with the date 22 September 1910.'*

He then makes the statement: *'The five dots stand for Alice or for her initials A S C S-W.'*

He adds: *'Edward Elgar and Alice Stuart-Wortley were souls in harmony as far as his music was concerned and this understanding was one of deep affection involving no disloyalty or infidelity to either of the other marriage partners. To a man of Elgar's poetic and sensitive imagination such a relationship was a strong emotional stimulus and it is one more example of Alice Elgar's noble character that where lesser women might have harboured groundless jealousies she interpreted the situation correctly because she understood her husband's nature.'*

This may be true concerning the extent of their relationship but he cites no evidence to support what he had written and the people on whom he had passed such a judgement were long dead by the time he came to write his book. So perhaps his statements should be viewed more as his own opinion and speculation rather than definitive *fact*.

However his sober judgement is certainly in keeping with what evidence we *do* have, rather than that of others.

The romantic nature of the concerto is of course the reason for all the speculation. But speculation when it becomes flights of romantic fancy can be a dangerous thing to do and of course over the years there have been all sorts of suggestions that Elgar and Alice were having a love affair and that the violin concerto was in some respects *their* love child.

The fact remains that whatever Elgar's relationship with Alice may or may not have been – and here one must take into account what Elgar, for his part, might have *wanted* it to have been – there is not a shred of evidence that it was any more than a long standing and doubtless very close friendship.

After all, back in those days men and women could enjoy close and even intimate friendships without the hint or suspicion of any clandestine activities. It was only in more modern times, encouraged by the innuendoes and exposures of the tabloid media that we began to see scandal within virtually every high profile relationship.

As far as Elgar and Alice Stuart-Wortley was concerned, there are a number of very strong indicators which suggest that their friendship was no more than just that.

For a start there is the mere existence of the considerable correspondence between them.

These letters were donated by Alice to Elgar's daughter, after Elgar died in 1934 – therefore making them public - so there was hardly any attempt at concealment. The correspondence also included Elgar's wife, and Alice Stuart-Wortley's husband, Sir Charles.

The Stuart-Wortley's marriage remained solid until he died in 1926, and it follows that if any hint of scandal had emerged it would have had a catastrophic effect not only on their marriage, but also Elgar's, and even more importantly, Sir Charles' standing in Victorian and Edwardian Society. He was, after all, a Member of Parliament and a Minister and the scandal of his wife being involved in some clandestine affair with the greatest composer of the age would surely have not only ended his parliamentary career but could easily have brought the government down.

In the cut and thrust world of Westminster there would have been no shortage of enemies who would have latched on to anything to achieve that end.

Alice's family nickname was *'Carrie'* and Elgar had addressed her only once by it. She objected and he never used that term again. It would seem therefore that Alice, drew a strict demarcation line between Elgar and too much familiarity.

But no further proof is needed, I think, than the way in which the dedication of Elgar's choral piece *'The Angelus'* written just before the Concerto, was handled.

This was his opus 64, and he dedicated it to her. Correspondence indicates that he sent his version of the dedication to her for approval. He wrote *'please look at the title carefully and tell me if I have it right and tell me how to amend it or to remove it altogether…anyway it would give me the greatest pleasure to put your beloved name on it if you <u>both</u> allow it.'*

We do not know what he proposed as it doesn't seem to have survived. But what he received by return was *her* version : *'Dedicated to Mrs Charles Stuart-Wortley'*, defining, I think, *exactly* how *she* saw her relationship.

The fact remains that we know so much today about the highly romantic nature of their relationship and the fact that he made it so plain the position she held in his affections, picking examples of *'windflowers'* (a type of anemone) from his garden and sending then to her - and indeed the fact that he was allowed by all parties on both sides to call her his *'Windflower'* at all. None of that was kept secret. Their relationship flourished throughout many years right up until their old age. So why make such a secret of her identity as the *'Soul'* if indeed it was she ?

After the deaths of Alice Elgar and Sir Charles, Elgar and his *Windflower* were free to marry, but they didn't. And one small incident in the 1920s shows she was clearly much more locked into Victorian tradition than Elgar had been. He offered to buy her a gramophone so that she could listen to the works she had supposedly inspired, but she refused to have any such new-fangled technology in her house.

So this woman, was still very much the formal Victorian lady – which renders the suggestion of clandestine derring-do somewhat illogical.

So, despite what might seem to be rock solid *'evidence'* that the *'soul'* of the concerto is Alice Stuart-Wortley, there can be doubts- which leads to the fourth and final candidate – and the supreme irony here is that Alice Stuart-Wortley *might* in fact provide a key to the *'soul'* being *her*.

She is Mrs Julia Worthington – and once again, as we have seen, she was one of the candidates, along with Helen Weaver and Mrs Nelson for being the subject of the anonymous Thirteen Variation in the *'Enigma Variations'*.

She was an American from New York, apparently very rich, a socialite who particularly favoured artists and creative people. The playwright W B Yeats for instance, once advised a relative who was travelling to America to seek her out as she provided a haven for artists – and then added, somewhat cryptically that she was a *'particular friend of the composer Elgar'*.

Julia was also divorced.

She conforms to the five letter requirement through her first name *Julia,* but more probably through her Elgarian nickname which was *'Pippa'* – a name derived from the long narrative poem by Robert Browning, *'Pippa Passes'* which tells the tale of a 14 year old Italian silk winder who, on the one day in the year that she gets off work, wanders around her local area singing a song which goes like this:

The year's at the spring,
And day's at the morn;
Morning's at seven;
The hill-side's dew-pearled;
The lark's on the wing;
The snail's on the thorn;
God's in His heaven—
All's right with the world!

The singing of the song has a profound effect on all the people that she encounters, and according to Elgar's close friend Ivor Atkins, Julia Worthington had the same effect. He said that the name was one of Elgar's finest inspirations as it exactly fitted Julia's charm, kindness and ability to bring out the best in all her friends and the light hearted and even mischievous influence on them.

She was apparently a mutual friend of Professor Samuel Sandford, of Yale University and it has been suggested that Elgar first met her on the voyage over to America in 1905 when Elgar and his wife sailed on the 'Deutschland' to accept an honorary degree from Yale and also to take part in his first tour of the USA. .

Julia's special connections to the Concerto arise from the fact that much of its composition took place in a villa at Careggi, Italy, when Elgar and his wife stayed with her.

It should be noted however, that parts of the concerto were also written at Alice Stuart-Wortley's home in Chelsea, Frank Schuster's Thames-side home 'The Hut' to say nothing of Elgar's own home in Hereford.

Julia's main claim is based on a rather strange incident which occurred at Elgar's home, shortly after the Violin Concerto was first performed.

The incident was chronicled by Dora Penny, the step daughter of one of Alice Elgar's lifelong friends who Elgar immortalised as the *'Dorabella'* variation in the *'Enigma Variations'*. At this time, she used to spend time at Hereford with the Elgars, and on one occasion shortly after the concerto came out she witnessed this curious episode. She subsequently published it in the first edition of her book *'Memories of a Variation'* which came out shortly after Elgar's death.

This is what she wrote: *'I heard the revised concerto played all through to me from a printed proof copy and I thought I had never heard anything more beautiful. What sadness and regrets, what high hopes and dreams was he describing ?*

'Alone in the study just before leaving for home I found a copy on the table and turned at once to pages which I had not noticed while I was busy with turning over.

'Having examined the title page I came next to the Spanish quotation on a page by itself. I knew no Spanish but the word 'alma' struck me – was it not 'soul' ? – and then the blank space with five dots caught my eye and a name immediately sprang to my mind.

'The door opened and the Lady [Elgar] came in. She came and stood by me, she saw what I was looking at and translated the Spanish sentence : 'herein is enshrined the soul of' then she went on to fill in the name – that of a personal friend – and asked me never to reveal it. I promised her that I never would. My guess was right.'

Dora kept her promise until 1946 when she brought out a second edition of the book when she said this:

'I think it may be conceded that there must be in practice a time limit to the value of such a promise as the one I gave to Lady Elgar in 1910. Writing as I do now in 1946 I feel that the limit in this case has been reached. Elgar's daughter agrees with me and it is with her full consent that I make known that the five dots in the Spanish quotation have concealed the identity of Mrs Julia H Worthington, a most charming and kind American friend. She was known to intimate friends by another name also of five letters and I cannot say for definite whether the composer had this name or her first Christian name in mind. Nor does this matter; the gap is now filled.'

Once again we have the whole matter being the subject of sworn promises that the name should never be revealed. One is bound to ask why, considering Julia was apparently so closely associated with the Elgars at the time that Dora apparently managed to guess it was her even before Alice Elgar confirmed it ?

But there are also a number of other curious aspects to Julia.

In the first instance, despite the fact that she was hailed as a dear friend of the Elgars' throughout many years, and despite the fact that Elgar at one point wrote that they had received letters *'as usual'* from her, only a handful of her letters have survived - and to date not a single letter of Elgar *to* her has emerged.

Elgar's composition *'The Angelus'* which he dedicated to Alice Stuart-Wortley, was written at the Careggi villa, and the working manuscript contains an inscription in Elgar's hand on the front page: *'Mem:This used paper in return for fair paper: to J.W. –the spirit of Careggi, from E.E. May 1909.'*

So, is Julia Worthington the *'dark lady'* in Elgar's life ? Some might think that she certainly begins to fit the bill. Elusive, foreign, divorced and therefore dangerous, known to be a close confident though a person who constantly recedes into the mists of speculation, hardly any extant letters, and a person who is solemnly dubbed as the identity of the *'Soul'* by Alice Elgar in an extraordinary revelation which carried no further explanation as to why – and a romantic speculation by Dora Penny citing sadness, regrets, high hopes and dreams. And then a solemn requirement from Alice Elgar that the name should *never* be revealed.

Furthermore, Elgar appears to have had extensive contact with Julia but without the presence of his wife - and particularly during his second tour of America and his third and final tour in 1911 , upon which he embarked alone, accompanied only by his French valet Jaulnay.

A further unusual aspect to this is that publicly he loathed America. Letter after letter berates the place, the weather, the people, the towns and cities - yet after what appears to have been a dismal encounter with the country in 1905 he chose to embark on two further tours there - but didn't set foot in America again after Julia Worthington had died in 1913.

When he finished his third and final tour, and a few days before he set sail across the Atlantic both he and Julia sent a joint postcard to a mutual English friend.

Elgar wrote simply: *'Love to you all, Edward Elgar'* but Julia added : *'Precious ones there - all Easter blessings - I sail with <u>him</u> on May 3. Your Pippa.'*

The fact that they travelled together across the Atlantic proved difficult to verify until the passenger list for the voyage came to light which strangely lists Julia under a different name – she's listed as *Janet* Worthington.

Another point which seems strange is that while the ship went initially to Fishguard they didn't get off the ship together – Julia apparently disembarked there and went to Paris, returning to the UK about a fortnight later, while Elgar stayed on board for another two days and disembarked at Liverpool citing inconvenient trains.

This may have been the case, yet there is even today a direct service from Fishguard to Hereford, where Elgar was living at the time. It also seems strange that he would shun the ability to travel direct from Fishguard even if it meant waiting for a couple of hours for a train, yet elect to stay on board the ship for a further two days, and end up even further away.

The *'fact'* about the trains, is quoted from Alice Elgar's diary. But Alice wasn't there – so the whole *'fact'* was actually as Elgar reported it to her

So were Elgar and Pippa Worthington lovers ? Or more importantly, were they *in love*, which would indicate a much more spiritual bonding ?

In the chapter on the *'Thirteen Variation'* I quoted the words of the eminent American conductor Leopold Stokowski when he spoke of his reminiscences in London as a young man, around 1902.

He had recalled seeing Elgar in the house of a beautiful American woman and stated that they were in love with each other, adding:

'Now Elgar was, first of all a great artist and then he was a really fine personality. He was married, he was true to his wife and yet he was in love with this girl and this was a great tragedy of Elgar's life...'

This can of course be dismissed as the somewhat misplaced remembrances of an old man. There is certainly no firm evidence to support his claims, and much of what links Elgar with Julia and any suggestion that they were lovers remains anecdotal.

It is certainly possible that such a person who by all accounts was bubbly, charming, beautiful and moreover rich could have attracted him – particularly as his wife Alice, despite her remarkable lifelong devotion to him, was hardly any of these things.

It is also possible that Elgar had several if not many liaisons – so the Mrs Nelson story might also be true.

In this regard, much store is made in some circles about an incident in 1915 when Alice described a play she had recently seen when she said: *'The only play in which a woman has the sense to say 'Nothing would make me believe it (a tale about her husband), even if it were proved I would not believe it'. I clapped and was joined by someone.'*

This would of course tally very much with Elgar's own statement of 1899 *'... a woman's not worth a damn who won't put up with everything except ineptitude and crime.'*

Alice Elgar, coming from gentry stock would certainly have been brought up in such a tradition – so it is quite possible that, as long as matters could never come to public attention, she might easily have accepted that as long as she was never officially made aware of her husband's behaviour, or the story otherwise *'got out'* and caused a scandal, it would not be a matter for either discussion or her reaction to it.

This, would certainly not have been the case if Elgar had been involved in any love affair with Alice Stuart-Wortley, the wife of a Minister of the Crown - but it does open up the possibilities that he could have been in love with a divorced socialite living 3,000 miles away, where the hint of scandal would be virtually non-existent.

It could also provide an explanation for why Alice, in revealing Julia's name to Dora Penny, supplied it only under the terms of absolute secrecy, and made her swear never to reveal it.

However, there is that supreme irony, as I mentioned earlier, that in fact Alice Stuart-Wortley actually provides more circumstantial evidence that Julia Worthington *might* in fact be the elusive *'soul'* – and even more ironically it comes from the very nature of Alice's nickname of *'Windflower'*.

It is easy to see this as a supremely romantic symbol – it sounds like a term straight out of a poem by Keats or Shelley – furthermore in a book from Elgar's library he makes a point of underlining a passage which reads : *'And the windflowers that danced with the wind.'* Added to the fact that Elgar used to cut examples of the flowers and send them to Alice in some of his letters to her, it is the sort of thing which you cannot fail to believe was love personified.

But perhaps it is important to examine what exactly Elgar was *really* suggesting when he called her *'windflower'*.

The answer to that is contained in a letter he wrote to her in which he described the windflower or anemone nemorosa in a way which may suggest why he called her such. This is what he wrote : *'when the rain clouds drive up, the petals shut tight into a tiny tent as country folk tell <u>to shelter the little person inside.</u>'*

So perhaps Elgar was suggesting that the *windflower* was not so much an icon of *affection*, but more that of *protection* – and in this context, what would his *windflower* be protecting? His inner thoughts perhaps, and his inner emotions ? Perhaps so – but why would he look upon this person to fulfil such a role ?

The answer to that may lie in Alice's back story.
Read the various literature and it will doubtless tell you that Alice was the daughter of Sir John Everett Millais, the founder of the Pre-Raphaelite brotherhood – but it goes much deeper than that.
Millais had famously painted a portrait of the leading art critic John Ruskin, standing on a rock at the side of a tarn in Scotland.
What Ruskin didn't realise however was that during the time Millais was doing the painting, he was falling deeply in love with Ruskin's wife – Euphemia Gray – who subsequently left her husband, divorced him and then married Millais.
It is said that she had emerged from the experience emotionally scarred , and though she was apparently happy with Millais and had eight children by him, she suffered terribly at the hands of Victorian morality being prevented on account of being a divorced woman from attending many functions with her husband and in later life it is said she became hard and somewhat cynical.
The Pre-Raphaelites were like any artistic movement of the time, not particularly noted for their moral fortitude, and were certainly controversial in the Victorian society in which they flourished. Dickens for example loathed and detested everything Millais did.
Alice was growing up in that environment, and would have been well aware of the traumas which her parents suffered as a result of her mother's divorce.

So Alice Stuart-Wortley, more than anyone else in Elgar's circle was the one who knew first-hand the traumas and dangers that love can bring – and certainly the consequences in Victorian/Edwardian society of divorce.

If, in fact, Elgar was suffering the traumas of the heart – if the anecdote of Stokowski has any credence at all – then it is logical to assume that Elgar would have needed enormous emotional protection – and who better to provide that than someone he named after a flower that according to his country roots he knew had the ability *to protect the little person inside* ?

This could of course be no more than mere speculation, except for one thing – Alice Stuart Wortley definitely knew of Julia Worthington, and knew of her as *'Pippa'* – her correspondence with Elgar proves that without a shadow of doubt.

And there are references which are both curious, but doubtless referring to Julia.

Writing from York in 1909 to her he asks *'how far is it from York to New York do you know?* and again in another letter written about the same time, he comments: *'how wide the Atlantic seems some days'*.

Then there was an incident in Cornwall which also occurred at around this time. Elgar embarked on a motoring tour with his friend Frank Schuster, and they were accompanied by Alice Stuart-Wortley and her sister.

When they got to Land's End, the weather was atrocious, but Elgar insisted on getting out of the car, walking out to sea and standing on the furthest south-west facing rock he could find, and stood there blowing a kiss across the Atlantic to Julia Worthington.

Such an action might naturally have seemed strange to the rest of the occupants in the car – especially if one of them, Alice Stuart-Wortley, was his clandestine lover. It is logical to consider that she would be wondering what on earth he was doing. It would seem much more likely however, that Alice Stuart Wortley, her sister and Frank Schuster knew *exactly* what he was doing.

At this point it is worthwhile introducing another character into this story. Elgar's friend and confident Nicholas Kilburn.

Kilburn was an industrial magnate from Bishop Auckland in the North East. His company manufactured pumps for the mines and heavy industry in the north east, but his greatest love was music and in this regard he founded three important music societies in Sunderland, Middlesbrough and Bishop Auckland.

He was a progressive and particular champion of English music and gave many very early performances of Elgar's works.

Elgar had a close friendship with him and on many occasions shared confidences that he did not share with his more local entourage. Kilburn was a very sage mentor and one Elgar knew he could trust – his knowledge of music was a great advantage, but, as he was living hundreds of miles away, it is logical to assume that Elgar may have felt confident that he could share matters with Kilburn without any risk that they might be divulged.

Shortly after the first performance of the Concerto, Kilburn staged a performance, and afterwards he wrote sending Elgar press reviews. But then he asked him to explain the meaning of the elusive Spanish inscription.

Elgar replied – providing what probably constitutes the *only* translation he ever gave himself:

'Here, or more emphatically <u>in here</u> is enshrined or (simply) enclosed – buried is perhaps [*'more'* crossed out] *too definite*

<u>*The soul of ...?*</u>

The final 'de' leaves it indefinite as to sex or rather gender.

Now guess.'

It would also seem plausible that Kilburn *did* guess as there is no evidence he ever asked again, but it may be significant that this translation was provided for this particular friend.

After all, if you are creating a mystery but you are not prepared to solve it – to the extent of taking its solution to the grave – but you are prepared to give someone, who you could trust implicitly like Kilburn, some sort of clue, then it is logical to assume that the person to whom you give that clue should be able to solve the mystery as a result.

It simply wouldn't work if you were giving a clue to someone who had not a shred of knowledge about what on earth you were talking about.

So, if this is the case then it pre-supposes that Kilburn must have had sufficient knowledge to guess the answer – particularly as in Elgar's letter he drew attention, by doubly underlining the words *'The Soul Of'* rather than anything else – and in fact in this letter he actually uses the three dots rather than five – indicating that the underlined words were the important element of this without drawing attention to a five letter word.

If this line of thinking is correct, Kilburn must have known whoever Elgar was referring to.

So did Kilburn know any of the four candidates discussed in this chapter ?

There is no evidence he knew anything of Helen Weaver – after all, she had long gone before he even got to know Elgar. It seems doubtful he would have had any knowledge of Mrs Nelson either.

As far as Alice Stuart-Wortley is concerned, there appears to be no evidence linking them. They lived in different circles both socially and geographically.

But what about Julia Worthington ?

In this case, there is certainly a connection.

Kilburn's business traded internationally and one of his most important business associates in America was the International Steam Pump Company, the President of which was *Charles Campbell Worthington* - Julia's estranged husband .

There is no doubt that Pippa was a particular friend of Nicholas Kilburn and his wife. The few letters in her hand which appear to have survived were written to the Kilburns and in a letter from Elgar to Kilburn dated September 2nd 1909 Elgar urges Kilburn to attend a party and makes a point of saying *'...Mrs Worthington will be there ...'*

Furthermore, the postcard Elgar and Julia wrote from New York when they were about to embark on their transatlantic voyage - *was sent to Kilburn.*

So it would follow that the only identity out of the four candidates whom Kilburn had the ability to derive was Julia Worthington – he simply didn't know the rest.

But there is one further very curious matter concerning this elusive Spanish inscription.

The manuscript full score of the concerto is deposited in the British Library. But the Spanish inscription *does not appear at all at the head of the work. It is simply not there.*

It would seem therefore that the quotation – the very thing which has inspired all this speculation for more than a century, was actually added in the proof stage of the printed score – might suggest that its very inclusion had to be concealed until the last minute. And if so – concealed from whom ?

So what conclusion can be drawn from all of this ?

It would seem logical to discount the first two candidates – as far as Helen Weaver is concerned, she was a girl who was part of a brief love affair in the early 1880s and it seems illogical that she could possibly be immortalised as the central character in a violin concerto written 30 years later. As for Mrs Nelson, and her daughter – it would seem improbable that they would have meant that much to Elgar, if indeed the story has any truth in it.

But what of the other two ? Was he in love with either of them ? Why did he call Alice Stuart-Wortley such a romantic name as *'windflower'* ? Was he deeply in love with her as some suggest ? Or was she a vital protector of his inner thoughts and emotions as his definition of *windflower* suggested ? Or was he in fact in love with a beautiful American called Julia Worthington ? Or is this nothing more than mere conjecture ?

There has been much speculation and theorising over the decades - theories, both sensible, and downright ridiculous, but my own belief for what it is worth is that the soul of the concerto *is* as stated by Lady Elgar to Dora Penny, Julia Worthington. And that this is a simple story of a love, deeply felt, which could never express its name.

Not only is the fact that Lady Elgar is supposed to have stated unequivocally that it was her – there is the fact that its revelation in 1946 was authorised by Elgar's daughter – and she was such a protector of the flame of her father's propriety that she would surely have prevented its revelation had it not been true.

There is also Dora's claim that she had already guessed the solution before being told with the elusive comment *'What sadness and regrets, what high hopes and dreams was he describing ?'*

Then there is the Kilburn connection and the speculation that he could only have followed Elgar's clues and guessed the solution if he had known the person to whom it referred. And the only one of these four women that he actually *did* know was Julia Worthington.

If in fact this is the case, and the whole mystery is founded in a deeply felt love that he could never reveal it might have resonance with other factors at around this time.

When he wrote his next great work, his Second Symphony, he headed the score with a quotation from Shelley: *'Rarely, Rarely, Commest Thou Spirit of Delight.'*

And it was also about this time that he wrote a Partsong which he dedicated to Julia, the words reading:

'Deep in my soul that tender secret dwells
Lonely and lost to light for evermore
Save when to thine my heart responsive swells
Then trembles into silence as before'

In 1912 he weaved a theme from the concerto into his choral work *'The Music Makers'* to the words: *'in our dreaming and our singing a little apart'*

There is also the texts of the rather curious song cycle he wrote at about the same time as he was composing the Concerto. It was first performed at the Jaeger memorial concert in January 1909 and he said it would eventually comprise six songs, but he only ever completed three – and at the concert, they were sung out of order – number 5 first then 3 then 6.

He also made particular reference in the programme notes that although the songs were sung by the soprano Muriel Foster at the concert, they ought really to have been sung by a man.

The words he set went like this, and some might feel that they had a particular significance in this context:

*Once in another land
Ages ago
You were a queen and I
I loved you so
Where was it that we loved
Ah, do you know
Do you know…
What it some golden star
Hot with romance
Was it in Malabar
Italy, France ?
Did we know Charlemagne
Dido, perchance ?*

*But you were a Queen
and I fought for you then
How did you honour me -
More than all men
More than all men
Kissed me upon the lips
Kiss me again*

*Have you forgotten it
All that we said ?
I still remember though
Ages have fled
Whisper the word of life –
"Love is not dead."*

Oh soft was the song in my soul and soft beyond thought were thy lips
And thou wert mine own and Eden re-conquered was mine
And the way that I go is the way of thy feet and the breath that I breathe
It hath being from thee and life from the life that is thine

Adieu ! and the sun goes a wearily down
The mist creeps up o'er the sleepy town
The white sails bend to the shuddering mere
And the reapers have reaped and the night is here

Adieu ! and the years are a broken song
The right grows weak in the strife with wrong
The lilies of love have a crimson stain
And the old days never with come again

Adieu !
Sometime shall the veil between
The things that are and that might have been
Be folded back for our eyes to see
And the meaning of all be clear to me.

Julia Worthington died from cancer in early June 1913. On March 16th, Kilburn wrote a long letter to Elgar saying that he had heard that Elgar had been very unwell adding: *'We must look up & then in proportion to our so varied capacities by an eternal law of life, there will be vouchsafed to us a sufficiency & fulfilment beyond even our highest hopes. P.s. we were grieved beyond measure at the news about Mrs Worthington. Has anything further been heard?'*

Which received this reply on March 26th
'You say we must look up? To What? To Whom? Why? You say: The mind bold and independent the purpose free must not think must not hope – Yet it seems sad that the only quotation I can find to fit my life comes from the Demons chorus! A fanciful summing up!'

Shortly afterwards he wrote *'Sospiri'* perhaps his most heart rending piece, and, as a biographer noted: *'Many of Elgar's letters surviving from this time are dull with unfulfillment – or with darkness made vivid by a single flash of old insight.'* And in one of those letters – to Rosa Burley – he wrote: *'Spring is the saddest season of the year if you do not take what is offered to you & only yearn for the things which are far off.'*
And in another letter to Kilburn bearing in mind that Julia was the 'spirit of Careggi' he says : *'I dream of Italy and all the things that cannot be...'*

So for my part I do believe that Elgar was deeply in love with Julia Worthington and that the circumstances of that relationship was the essence of tragedy. What could be more tragic than to fall deeply in love with someone

and know that you can never really take your relationship to a satisfying conclusion ?
I do believe that he found a kindred spirit in Alice Stuart-Wortley and through her he could confide the inner traumas that the situation was causing him. She was the *windflower* which protected the little person inside against the storm.

But this is my *belief.* We will never know the real solution of this mystery. Elgar made sure that he took it with him to the grave. Everything that has been said on this matter has been on a basis of speculation, interpretation based mostly on circumstantial evidence.

But such a solution, as I have discussed, might explain why so many commentators who knew Elgar personally referred to his life being troubled and tragic without providing any real explanation as to why it was so.

THE DREAM OF GERONTIUS

Many consider Elgar's 1900 choral work *'The Dream of Gerontius'* to be his masterpiece. But it is also as much known for the disaster of its first performance - one of the most infamous of all events in the history of classical music.

It's a setting of a long narrative poem by Cardinal John Henry Newman, a leading figure in the re-establishment of the Roman Catholic faith in the UK.

Newman had originally been a Church of England priest but during the mid-1800s became disenchanted with his faith and despite enormous social pressure at the time converted to Catholicism. He is now revered as a Saint.

His poem, *'The Dream of Gerontius'* was written in 1865 and tells of the journey of the soul of an old man, through death and into a very Catholic interpretation of the after-life, where he meets his Guardian Angel, encounters demons bent on dragging souls to hell, and then faces judgement by God. In the final section he descends into Purgatory where he pays for his sins on Earth before eventually ascending into Heaven.

Many consider that the literary merits of the poem are far from the finest, and Newman himself is said to have screwed up the manuscript and thrown it into a bin before one of his junior priests retrieved it. However, the metaphysical nature of the work struck great accord with Victorian society and it became a very popular publication.

Elgar was given a copy of the poem as a present when he married in 1889, and being Catholic himself, the philosophy of the poem resonated with him to the extent that he spent the next ten years wrestling with the idea of setting it to music.

The great Czechoslovakian composer Antonin Dvorak had also considered setting it, but, as the story goes, when he heard that Elgar was attempting to do just that, he withdrew.

The opportunity finally to compose *'Gerontius'* arrived when the Birmingham Triennial Festival commissioned Elgar to write the chief new work for their 1900 event.

Initially, he had no idea what to do. As he wrote to his publishers, Novellos, shortly after the offer had been made to him:

'...we settled, verbally, that I am to have the principal place in the Birmingham Festival...now I have to consider the subject which must be sacred: can you suggest anything?'

Novellos replied suggesting that he should write something which could be easily performed by amateur choirs – and once again suggested he write something along the lines of works produced by the great master of light classical music Sir Edward German.

Elgar declared that he would not write anything along those lines, but the subject of the work he would eventually write eluded him – until just before the Birmingham Festival Committee Chairman came to see him to finalise the arrangements on New Year's Day 1900.

Just why he didn't immediately seize upon the opportunity of setting a poem which had been in his mind for ten years is not altogether clear, but undoubtedly the idea of using Cardinal Newman's poem as a basis for this new great work had risks which up to this time Elgar had been careful to avoid.

He had made his reputation on large scale choral works produced for provincial musical festivals which were the life-blood of classical music outside London at the time. In the main, he had been careful to avoid religious subjects, opting instead for Scandinavian mythology in his *'Scenes from the Saga of King Olaf'* and Celtic history in *'Caractacus'*.

By setting non-religious subjects he avoided any controversy or confusion with his own faith. Catholicism, though generally accepted, was still regarded with suspicion in many circles of Victorian society, and it would have been unwise to create any difficulties which might otherwise arise.

Setting a poem which was unequivocally Catholic in nature, had references throughout to Catholic doctrine, was unquestionably taking a risk. Yet circumstances in his own life may have finally made him decide to carry out what he had always intended.

Just before the Chairman of the Birmingham Festival Committee came to Malvern to finalise the commission for the new work, Elgar's father, William Henry Elgar fell gravely ill, as Elgar wrote to a friend:

'I was very glad to get your note which was and is cheering in a time of depression. All goes wrong ! I omitted all Christmas greetings: my dear old father is hovering between death and life and I have been expecting the final news anytime during these last few days. My own troubles are all squalid and uninteresting even to myself.'

It is quite possible therefore that this may have been the catalyst for his final decision. Perhaps the events depicted in the poem – an old man dying and his soul travelling into the afterlife – resonated with his own feelings at a time of desperate grief in his own household, and therefore the work he eventually produced may have been intended as a requiem in memory of his father.

In the event William Henry was to recover and lived for another five years, but at the time Elgar made his decision, as indicated in his letter, he really did *believe* his father was about to die, and had no reason to speculate that he would continue to live for so long.

If this was the case, then it will explain why he threw so much emotional weight into the composition of the work. Here are two letters he wrote during the composition which show how he felt:

'...I am at work at Gerontius ...I like what I have done – I am bold & have shirked nothing – I've made my own 'atmosphere' & stuck to it – Much modern music annoys me thus: when we come to the 'high' situation the composers too often let the voice recite on one note- this seems to me that the musician confesses his art is unworthy – perhaps it shows the composer is 'unworthy' – I don't know – but I do know that I won't write so – if I fail it's not the fault of music per se – but of me !'

'...my work is good to me & I think you will find Gerontius far beyond anything I've yet done – I <u>like</u> it – I am not suggesting that I have risen to the heights of the poem for one moment – but on our hillside night after night looking across our 'illimitable' horizon I've seen in thought the Soul go up & have written my own heart's blood into the score...'

And at the end of the finished score he wrote these words, quoted from John Ruskin: *'This is the best of me; for the rest, I ate, and drank, and slept, loved and hated, like another: my life was as the vapour and is not; but this I saw and knew; this, if anything of mine, is worth your memory.'*

In the event, the first performance of *'Gerontius'* became, as we shall see, one of the most infamous events in the whole history of classical music – and it is most possible that Elgar's personal resonation with the work may explain why, when its first performance was so decidedly under par, he went into melt-down.

The generally accepted reason for the disaster is that the performance was, well, appalling. The main blame lay with the chorus which, by all accounts was badly out of tune at times, and generally ill-disciplined, with the result that the whole thing added up to one of the worst events in musical history.

This may have been the case – but simply to lay the blame on a bad set of singers is hardly enough to explain the reasons *why* the performance was so atrocious. These are much less easy to define, and it is true that there were factors for which Elgar, himself, was decidedly to blame.

In the first instance, Elgar did not begin any work until after his meeting with the Birmingham Chairman in early January 1900 – with the performance set for early October of that year, hardly enough time was allowed for the work to be properly prepared for performance.

He eventually finished the score in August – leaving just ten weeks for the parts to be printed, proofed, corrected and finally published, before any of the performers actually had sight of the work at all.

Another important factor was the way in which rehearsals were conducted in those days.

The chorus – all amateur singers – rehearsed in Birmingham. The orchestra, when they finally received their parts, rehearsed in London, and the three soloists needed for the production rehearsed whenever and wherever their other commitments allowed.

Elgar was warned by one of his friends, Nicholas Kilburn, a seasoned choral conductor, that all would not be well. As soon as he got sight of the work he wrote urgently: '...*for such a work's rendering dare we hope for that which is worthy? Alas! I fear, I fear! Were I dictator, state funds should provide the means full & adequate, and a stately Cathedral, & I wd. summon <u>only</u> musicians, <u>only</u> artists to listen, & <u>not once</u> only; and thus should justice be done.*'

Elgar also decided to allow the Festival Chief Conductor, the great Wagnerian conductor Hans Richter, who had given the premiere of the *'Enigma Variations'* to conduct the first performance. This was considered unusual at the time – when it was assumed that all new works would be conducted by their composers.

As one of the newspapers commented: *'it is to be regretted that Mr Elgar has not accepted the position which was his by precedent. With a real live chorus master to prepare the choristers, if the musician can compose music worth hearing at a festival, he can direct his forces. Given that ability, he should neither be robbed, nor suffered to rob himself, of the honour.'*

Fate also played a part because the preparations received yet another body blow. The chorus master Charles Swinnerton Heap, a young man who firmly understood Elgar's music having been heavily involved in performances of some of his earlier Choral works, died suddenly and was replaced as an emergency measure at the last minute by the 70 year old William Stockley.

Stockley, who in fact had given Elgar some of his earliest chances as a composer when he performed some of his first orchestral works in the 1880s, has long been unfairly criticised for not understanding Elgar's music, and thus being responsible for what happened.

Stockley was from an older generation and was far more used to the works of the past, such as the oratorios of Bach or Handel which feature individual stand-alone items or *'numbers'* that make up the whole.

But it is decidedly unfair to condemn a man who was introduced to such a radical new work and given but a few weeks to prepare the chorus in time for its performance.

'Gerontius' was, without question, some of the most complicated and radical music that had been encountered at the time. Furthermore, unlike oratorios of the past, it was written with seamless action, like an opera, and thus

made demands of the chorus which had never been encountered before.

Another factor was the enormous programme of works which were packed into the Festival's three days. Apart from *'Gerontius'* the Birmingham chorus also had to learn Mendelssohn's *'Elijah'*, Bach's *'St Matthew Passion'*, Handel's *'Messiah'*, Brahms' *'German Requiem'*, sections from Handel's *'Israel in Egypt'*, Dvorak's *'The Spectre's Bride'*, Sir Hubert Parry's *'De Profundis'* and another new work, Coleridge Taylor's *'Song of Hiawatha'*. The orchestra also had to tackle a number of purely orchestral pieces.

The enormity of the task involved in rehearsing such a demanding programme was not lost on one of the leading musical publications of the time, *The Musical Standard*, in an article written just four days before *'Gerontius'* was due to be performed:

'It is late in the day to speak of the rehearsal arrangements at Birmingham. It was stated, not officially it is true, that both 'Messiah' and 'Elijah' were to be rehearsed otherwise than chorally but we note that neither of these masterpieces figures in the printed order of rehearsals although the selections from 'Israel in Egypt' do. That is rather a pity as no festival has yet taken place at which the fashion of giving these familiar works without full rehearsal has not had bad results – at least if one expects perfection.

'But when two novelties 'The Dream of Gerontius' and 'The Song of Hiawatha' are in the programme, which also contains such exacting choral works as Brahms' 'Requiem', Bach's 'St Matthew Passion' and Dvorak's 'Spectre's Bride' all to be rehearsed with soloists, chorus and orchestra <u>within the space of a full day, an evening and a morning</u> it is difficult to understand how time could be found for the rehearsal of familiar pieces.

'Still, in listening to the orchestra trying over the orchestral music of 'The Dream of Gerontius' and afterwards to the soloists running through their parts and with the knowledge that the only full rehearsal of soloists, chorus and orchestra will take place at Birmingham this Saturday afternoon when the work is bracketed with Sir Hubert Parry's 'De Profundis' one could not keep feeling strongly once again that the rehearsal arrangements at our festivals entirely prevent them taking the stand they should.

'How all this is to be obtained from the single rehearsal at Birmingham, we do not understand, but rest in the placid hope, that it will be 'all right on the night'.'

The *Sunday Times* commented on yet another deficiency in its preparation: *'The full score is said to be the most complicated that an Englishman has ever written. It was only available practically at the last moment for the purposes of the analytical notes and the preliminary band rehearsal held at Queen's Hall* [London] *on*

Monday. As a matter of fact, Dr Richter had never set eyes upon the score until last Sunday evening.'

And another commentator paid tribute to the orchestral players who, it seems, only a few days before the first performance *sight read* the music, because they had only received it that day.

The first joint rehearsal took place on September 28th – five days before the premier – when an incident, often considered a major contributor to the disastrous premiere, occurred – and this time Elgar was very much to blame.

He had attended that rehearsal and during one part, the *'Demon's Chorus'* he asked Richter if he could address the choir. As a reporter who was there wrote: *'And then the composer made matters worse at the final rehearsal by putting up the backs of the choir. He told them that their singing was 'all wrong' and the Chorus of Demons was sung as if it were a drawing room ballad.'* But the article continued: *'The fact is that the choir were overworked and they had not a conductor in Dr Richter who could inspire them with new life at the last moment.'*

Another reporter wrote: *'Mr Elgar's outburst though justified enough by the performance was ill advised. It took the spirit out of the singers without giving any suggestion as to what he wanted.'*

It was an incident that angered so many members of the chorus that some even wrote to the papers about it after Elgar's death, 34 years later.

The fundamental disagreement between composer and performers could not have been worse. On the one hand was an emotional musician, desperate for so many reasons to see the work he had regarded as the best he had ever produced, performed at least adequately.

On the other hand there was a group of hard working amateur singers, drawn in the main from Birmingham and the Black Country who would probably have been working six days a week and for whom singing was their only libation from a Victorian work regime that was harsh and unremitting. They had also been expected to rehearse a daunting number of some of the longest and most complicated choral works in the repertoire – and *'Gerontius'* was the most radical piece they had ever encountered.

It was inevitable that these hardened Midlands souls resented the artistic outburst of someone that they probably regarded as having never done a real day's work in his life

Many years later a female member of the chorus wrote that Richter had wandered about imploring them to do their best, *'for the work of this English genius'* but by that time the chorus members had had enough.

As one of the reviews commented: '

'A more perfunctory rendering of a new work it has never been my lot to listen to at a big Festival. The tenors began flat in the very first semi-chorus and set an example of doubtful intonation that prevailed throughout most of the many in the cantata where awkward intervals and trying dissonances lay a trap for these unwary choristers. Nay more; their attack was rarely unanimous and their rendering of passages requiring the most delicacy often offended the ear by a grating harshness of tone and slovenliness of phrasing.

'In a word, a spirit of hesitancy permeated the entire performance and wrought material harm at its birth to a composition which demands in a peculiar degree the absence of those distracting influences which accompany a faulty interpretation. So much, apparently for the value of the extra day's rehearsal which Dr Richter was in such pains to secure in order to make all safe!'

After it was all over, Elgar wrote to his friend August Jaeger at his publishers Novellos one of his most famous and often quoted letters:

'As far as I'm concerned music in England is dead...I have worked hard for forty years & at the last, Providence denies me a decent hearing of my work: so I submit – I always said God was against art and I still believe it. Anything obscene or trivial is blessed in this world and has a reward – I ask for no reward – only to live & to hear my work...I have allowed my heart to

open once – it is now shut against every religious feeling and every soft, gentle impulse for ever...'

And ever since, the standard belief is that *'Gerontius'* failed so badly at its first outing that it almost sank without trace. Only a masterly performance by the Germans at the Lower Rhine Festival in Dusseldorf two years later revived its fortunes and ever since *'Gerontius'* has been regarded as one of the greatest choral masterpieces in classical music.

This belief, based largely on the undeniable fact that the first performance *was* under par, and Elgar's reaction to the whole episode in his letter to Jaeger, is not exactly accurate however.

Judging on the reactions of the critics who attended, while they accepted the short comings of the performance, they nevertheless raved about the work itself.

Here is one, that sums up the general reaction:

'I am about to speak words which may seem exuberant and enthusiastic; but I have thought over them carefully before setting them down for the public eye, and I will venture to say that since the death of Wagner, no finer composition (I am quite remembering Tchaikovsky and his great symphonies) has been given to the world. I am proud that Mr Elgar is an Englishman, for his has justified Purcell's early career; in a word he has produced a genuine masterpiece.

And here is another: *'I have no hesitation in saying that the composer of 'Gerontius' is a genius of whom England ought to be proud'*

One little known fact about performances at that time is that as far as religious works were concerned, the audience were under the strictest requirement not to applaud at the end. It was regarded as a sacred homage.

In the case of *'Gerontius'* however, this is what happened, in the words of yet another journalist who was there:

'At the close there were loud calls for the composer, who did not appear for some minutes but eventually was the recipient of an enthusiastic ovation.'

Elgar had been sitting at the back of the auditorium, no doubt with the intention of making a quick exit if matters had gone as badly as he had feared. His passage to the platform, according to one anecdote, was blocked by a member of the audience, taking part in the standing ovation, who told him to stop pushing *'because we're waiting for Elgar to arrive'*.

It is also the case that *'Gerontius'* was not the only work to receive a bad performance at the Festival.

The *Sunday Times* commented: *'The crisis came early in the proceedings. In Sir Hubert Parry's 'De Profundis', we were rudely awakened to the fact that something was wrong. Either the choir did not know the work or it was unequal to the exigencies of twelve-part choral writing.*

It got astray at the outset and was more than once so near disaster that I for one expected the genial composer to throw down his baton in sheer despair.

'This unpleasant experience augured ill for the 'safe delivery' of Mr Edward Elgar's still more exacting contribution on the following morning. Here indeed rumour had already prepared us for serious shortcomings. The final rehearsal of 'The Dream of Gerontius' had, it was said, been so far the reverse of satisfactory, that the composer lost patience with the chorus and told them in good plain English that they either knew nor understood his music. And this the actual performance proved to be the case.

'The very next morning in the St Matthew 'Passion' we heard passages blurred, sung out of tune, and given what a want of steadiness and precision worthy of a fourth-rate provincial choral society.''

The first performance of *'The Dream of Gerontius'* though legendary in the annals of classical music, is, as always with historical events, not exactly how it is presented in so many accounts.

Subsequent performances by the Germans and then in England – this time with choruses that had been properly prepared and with soloists who were used to singing in opera, have cemented its place as one of the major masterpieces of the choral repertoire – and one regarded by some as Elgar's finest utterance – or as he put it himself *'This was the best of me.*

WHEN ELGAR TOPPED THE BILL AT THE MUSIC HALLS

Imagine the scene. It is October 1903 and you are sitting in the packed auditorium of the Birmingham Town Hall on a day which has long been previewed as being by far the most exciting moment in the Birmingham Festival that year.

In the audience are some of the finest celebrities of the age, including the rising local politician Neville Chamberlain – later to become the Prime Minister.

On the stage is a large orchestra and an even larger chorus, all expectantly waiting for the arrival of six of the country's best known principal singers, and their conductor, Dr Edward Elgar.

They arrive, take up their positions on stage and Elgar stands on the podium, raising the baton in his hand. The audience grows silent.

Then the sounds of the opening bars of the magnificent opening of *'The Apostles'* begins to pervade the air.

It is one of the most memorable moments in the history of music in Britain.

Fast forward in time to November 1910.

Now you are sitting in a similarly packed auditorium but this time it is the Queen's Hall, London – one of

Europe's most important concert venues – and before you is a large orchestra awaiting the arrival of the greatest violinist in the world, Fritz Kreisler.

He appears on stage, looking strangely nervous, as though the importance of the moment is affecting him, together with Sir Edward Elgar, who will conduct the world premiere of his Violin Concerto - an event which the musical world has been anticipating with great excitement for almost a year.

At the end, you join the rest of the audience in rising up with cheers of acclamation having heard one of the finest violin concertos ever written. It is a moment which you will never forget.

Now fast forward another seven years. It is now the autumn of 1917, in some of the darkest days of the First World War.

Now you are sitting in a provincial music hall. As the curtain goes up, on stage have arrived four men, dressed up as 'jolly jack tars', against a theatrical backdrop suggesting they are having a few beers in a harbour-side tavern on the coast.

A rag-bag of a band, the best that can be mustered under the circumstances, given that most of the country's musicians are serving at the front, is assembled in the pit, and there to join them is no less a figure than the great composer Sir Edward Elgar himself.

He raises his baton in the limelight, the band strikes up and the singers commence the latest performance of his song cycle *'The Fringes of the Fleet'*, as part of the nationwide tour of a show which proved the hit of the season when it opened in the early summer at London's Coliseum Theatre.

In the programme you're holding in your hand there are some jovial cartoons showing scenes from the production together with a narrative poem which begins:

'Four Rough and Ready Sailor men

You see upon the stage

Though no-one in particular

Today they're all the rage

They're called the 'Fringes of the Fleet'

And tell you all in song

About their life upon the Sea

In language rather strong

They started out upon their trip

Upon a day in June

('Twas Rudyard Kipling wrote the words

And Elgar set the tune)

Sir Edward Elgar, I should say

That gallant chevalier

Of whom the ladies all exclaim

'Oh, isn't he a dear!''

You are there in response to adverts in the local press which have enthusiastically invited you to *'Come and hear Sir Edward Elgar conduct his music <u>in person</u>'.*

Later in the programme you will be entertained by such acts as *Pierce and Roslyn* in a whirl of melody, *Haslam & Lady* in their 'matrimonial burlesque' *'Smilestones'*, *Baisdon*, the talking comedy cyclist; *Ella Retford* the light comedy singer, made famous by her renditions of *'All the nice girls love a sailor'* and *'She's a lassie from Lancashire', Vera Caine* the female boxer, *Dr Nichols and Company* with their 'screaming farce' *'It's Up to You'* and of course, *Mademoiselle Dalmere's* table circus of rats, rabbits, and canaries.

The contrast in terms of Elgar's career seems stark. At the time, the musical world was bemused as to how someone regarded at the time as the greatest composer in the land, famous for his deeply serious Biblical oratorios, and a succession of orchestral masterpieces such as his *Violin Concerto*, the *'Enigma' Variations*, and his two symphonies, could be performing as the go-to act in a variety show performing in music halls up and down the country.

One correspondent, writing for the Leicester Illustrated Mercury, for example, wrote this: *'The appearance of the greatest of living English composers, Sir Edward Elgar, at the Leicester Palace this week, is an event of more than ordinary interest. Some folk of old-fashioned notions probably think that artistic dignity has received a rude shock through celebrated musicians having consented to perform at music-halls.'*

While another, from the Manchester Guardian when the show reached there had a slightly different opinion: *'Our tendency as a people to identify an artist too rigidly with his material has until quite recently prevented a full recognition of the personality of Sir Edward Elgar who is at the Manchester Hippodrome this week, conducting ('in person' as the theatre-posters state in careful detail) some of his own compositions.*

'We came to know Elgar first of all through his 'Gerontius' preferring it to other of his works, probably because of the inordinate national predilection for oratorio and it was generally taken for granted that the man who could write such super-earthly music as 'The Dream of Gerontius' must of necessity be himself unsubstantial and febrile. Consequently the surprise expressed in many quarters at his appearance and reception in the music-hall can be understood. But true Elgarians have always known our greatest composer – and he really stands with the very greatest – to be intensely human.

'Since 1914 it would seem Elgar has deliberately simplified his art and broadened it to a communal pattern in order to gain a point of contact with the people. The result has been some of the most inspiring patriotic music ever written. Elgar is the only English composer who has attempted fairly and squarely to tune his melody to the time and to serve his country by the expression of its convictions and emotions concerning the war. He could not wholly fulfil this task without venturing into the music-hall which is beloved of our soldiers and has become the place of all others for the expression of popular feeling.

'It was with no loss of dignity therefore but rather with a new accession of it that the composer of 'The Dream of Gerontius' came forward to conduct the meagre and too little competent orchestra at the Manchester Hippodrome yesterday in his setting of Kipling's war ballads. One felt he had become a follower of Dibdin and the older ballad writers who made the story of our country the pride of their music'.

So what was this work which caused such a dramatic change in Elgar's behaviour, and why did he embark on such a project at all ?

The answer can be found in two aspects of Elgar's character – the first is that at heart he was a jobbing musician. In his early life he had worked for more than 20 years, conducting local choirs and orchestra, playing and teaching violin as well as a variety of other instruments, and performed in all sorts of venues – even the local Lunatic Asylum, during the period when he was the resident Band Master.

To put it simply, music was his 'trade', and as such he had no superior airs and graces when it came to performing – being at one of Europe's most prestigious concert venues, at a Lunatic Asylum, or, as here, in a variety music hall.

And the key to his attitude was that it was guided by money. As long as the money was good, then he was quite happy to perform, and by 1917, he certainly needed money.

In 1912 Elgar and his family moved from the provincial surroundings of his home territory on the Welsh borders to a sumptuous mansion in an exclusive area of Hampstead, north London.

By this time he was in some demand as a conductor and the idea of the move was said to allow him to be nearer to the various London concert venues, but it is just as likely that his wife, Alice, was a driving force behind the whole thing.

After all, she had given up mansion house living in 1889 when she had married him and had spent the ensuing years of their marriage living in much more modest accommodation. So it would seem logical to assume that a move to a grand north London mansion would be the final achievement in a quest to return to the sort of living to which she had been so used in the first forty years of her life.

They called the place 'Severn House' – no doubt a title created by Elgar to provide a link with his *'sweet homeland of the borders'* he had left behind – and it is no exaggeration to suggest that Alice relished living there.

A reporter from the Daily Express reflected this in an article shortly after they had moved in: *'Lady Elgar, wife of the great composer, dispenses much informal hospitality at their beautiful home in Hampstead where one of the most striking features is the huge music room, where Sir Edward may sometimes be persuaded to sit at the grand piano on a Sunday afternoon and improvise for the pleasure of intimate friends who drop in for tea.*

'In the billiard room – billiards is one of Sir Edward's chief recreations – Lady Elgar has arranged a fascinating collection of wonderful trophies presented to her husband at the various musical festivals at which his works have been produced.

'Most attractive of all is the Blue Study – Lady Elgar's special pride – where carpet, chair-covers and hangings are all a lovely shade of deep blue, blue-bound books abound and some fine specimens of old blue Bristol glass give a note of glorious colour. Deep blue flowers are chosen and even the blotting paper in the wide writing pad is a deep shade of blue.'

She may have loved 'Severn House', but it is questionable whether Elgar himself was so keen.

In a letter to his friend, Rosa Burley with whom he cycled for miles in the countryside around Malvern he bemoaned the life he had left behind: *'Yes I remember all the sweetness of it – the syringa, then the beans and the limes. I suppose I shall never see it all again or cycle over the old places. How lovely the [Longdon] marsh must be – I envy you your seeing it & living in it all again. During the two moments I have spent in M[alvern] – all the people seem to disappear & only the eternal hills & all the memories of the old loveliness remains…'*

However, overriding all other considerations was the fact that 'Severn House' was a much more expensive house to run than any they had previously occupied, and Elgar had to face the realities of paying the bills.

As a result, Elgar had to pursue work which would ensure lucrative returns and in this regard he developed a relationship with Oswald Stoll, who headed the theatre syndicate which ran the London Coliseum in Central London, one of the country's most important music halls, and also controlled a number of music halls and theatres in the provinces.

Their first collaboration was in the Masque called 'The Crown of India' which |I discussed in a previous chapter and which ran in 1912 to celebrate the visit of George V and Queen Mary to India where he was crowned Emperor at the Delhi Durbar.

Elgar's involvement raised a few eyebrows in the musical establishment even then, as one of the papers commented: *'Noted composers as well as popular actors and playwrights are answering more and more to the demands of the variety theatre. Of late foreign composers, like Leoncavallo and Mascagni, have graced the conductor's chair in the music-hall, but it is a good many years since an English composer of the standing of Sir E Elgar has taken up the baton there.'*

The Masque however proved popular and laid a foundation for other projects in the West End. From Elgar's point of view it meant that he could earn good money from writing music which was hardly as taxing as the great oratorios or orchestral music of the past.

When war broke out in 1914, he was reluctant to write music for the war effort, mainly because the enemy was Germany, a country which he loved and which had been his favourite destination for holidays in his earlier days. He also owed a great deal to many Germans – not least the composer Richard Strauss who had put Elgar on the international map by praising him as the *'Meister'* of English music, and August Jaeger, his indefatigable champion at his publishers Novellos.

Nevertheless, after the atrocious treatment of Belgium by the German army in the early stages of the War, Elgar was persuaded to write three collaborative efforts with the Belgian poet Emile Camaarts which were performed in West End theatres. These amounted to orchestral accompaniments to rousing poetry written by Camaarts and declaimed by the poet himself in the first performances and then by actors.

Then in 1915 Elgar was invited to write some incidental music for a Christmas Children's play staged at the Kingsway Theatre, called *'The Starlight Express'*, written by Algernon Blackwood.

The play proved to be not the greatest success, but some of the music was recorded for the then fledgling Gramophone Company – which in itself laid the foundation for a lucrative source of income which was to last for the rest of Elgar's life.

So when in 1917, the invitation came in from the Stoll Syndicate to contribute to a summer variety show at the Coliseum, Elgar already had a good track-record for producing music for the West End.

The idea he came up with was to set four poems by Kipling which paid tribute to the activities of the small sea vessels operating around the shores of the country. This was already titled by Kipling *'The Fringes of the Fleet'*, and Elgar set about the idea with enthusiasm commenting in a letter that he had written the music in a *'broad salt-water style'*.

The settings were for four baritone singers, led by Charles Mott, one of the most famous singers of the day

– who had also starred in the earlier *'Starlight Express'* production.

The show was originally intended to run for only a week in July, but proved so popular that its London run was extended week after week and well into the autumn. Thereafter a touring production was put together that played at music halls throughout the country – and Elgar conducted every performance, twice nightly and matinees twice a week.

After the autumn provincial tour, it returned to the Coliseum for a run in November of that year. By this time, even the critics had been won over to the idea of a great classical composer performing in music halls.

The Era a well-known arts magazine of the time commented that it was *'one of the finest productions ever seen in the music-halls,'* and The Manchester City News felt that *'it is fitting that works so typically national in character should receive their first welcome in that great national meeting place of all classes, the music-hall. Posterity, in accord with present-day opinion will undoubtedly acclaim Elgar as the most typically English of all our great national composers.'*

But all was not well – and by the end of December, Kipling, unhappy at the production, put a stop to the performances and the physical pressure which Elgar had endured by conducting night after night began to take its toll on his health.

In view of what eventually happened, Elgar's must have severely regretted setting poetry by Kipling, rather than the work of a less high-profile poet, but there was nothing he could do.

His own bitterness at the turn of events was expressed in a letter to a friend: *'I fear the songs are doomed by R.K. he is perfectly stupid in his attitude.'*

Rumours began to circulate that he was unwell and some of these reached the press with one correspondent noting: *'There have been rumours of late, some of them rather alarming concerning the health of Sir Edward Elgar. I am more than pleased to hear there is no foundation for them whatever. Sir Edward has been ill, though not seriously and is now on his way to complete recovery.'*

This was not the case. He eventually was admitted to a nursing home and needed a prolonged period of recovery. The physical and mental toll on him – he was 60 years of age by this time – coupled with the sudden curtailment of a lucrative source of income brought him to his knees.

This effectively put an end to Elgar's career in the music halls, though he did return to working in the theatre during the 1920s, writing incidental music for two plays.

The notion of the country's greatest composer strutting the boards of provincial music halls in the company of comedy cyclists, female boxers and a table-top animal circus might seem a strange and bizarre episode in his career, and it might be fanciful to believe that somehow his career had nose-dived.

This was certainly not the case. During his convalescence, he retired to a remote country cottage, set in dense Sussex woodlands called *'Brinkwells'* and here he produced what many believe to be his greatest masterpieces – his three magnificent chamber works and his extremely popular 'Cello Concerto.

But it has always seemed to me that this episode when he effectively 'topped the bill' at the music halls, said so much about the fundamental character who was Edward Elgar.

As far as he was concerned performing on stage in Leicester, Nottingham, Manchester and the Chiswick Empire was no different to appearing in some of the great concert venues of the world. He was a musician and if the money for his performance was good enough he would certainly consider performing – in other words he carried none of the 'artistic superiority' and disdain that others might have possessed.

It was all to the pity for his finances that while the poet Rudyard Kipling had major reservations about his poetry being performed in lowly music halls, the great Sir Edward Elgar OM had no qualms about appearing twice nightly and twice a week at matinees conducting his settings of them.

THE MYSTERY OF ELGAR AND DELIUS

In 1933 Elgar, then aged 76, made a celebrated trip to France.

The visit was arranged by the Gramophone Company and its main purpose was to promote the recently made recording of his Violin Concerto with the 16 year old Yehudi Menhuin, via concerts in Paris.

Elgar, however expressed the wish that he also be allowed to visit his fellow composer Frederick Delius at his home at Grez-Sur-Loing, near Fontainbleau south of the French capital – and thereby hangs a tantalising mystery.

The notion of two such great names of English music meeting in the twilight of their days proved irresistible, particularly given the circumstances. Elgar, long retired from serious composition, and somewhat withdrawn from public life, was now largely regarded as an icon of a long-lost past, while Delius, living far away from England and by this time blind and paralysed, was equally enigmatic.

The visit aroused great interest from the press and the meeting, though private, was extensively covered. Fred Gaisberg, the Gramophone Company's legendary producer accompanied Elgar, and gave his own account to the Press.

'"There was something of pathos in that meeting,' he said. 'Yet I have never seen two men with so much joy at being together again. Both of them are old and one is blind and stricken with paralysis. Yet in the two hours that they were together they seemed completely to recapture their lost youth.'

Gaisberg then made this reference:

'They talked of happy days together at Leipzig, of concerts where they had listened together, and of music they had created and played to each other. They were really like a pair of boys.

'Sir Edward was immediately enthusiastic over his first aeroplane flight from London to Paris and he evolved with Delius a grandiose scheme so that they could fly round Europe together giving the greatest concerts that the world has ever known.

'Delius, although stricken as he is, retains all his brightness and he told Sir Edward that a new choral work upon which he has been engaged has almost been completed. Elgar, too, told him something of the music he was planning for the future and they talked of great figures of the past now dead. Delius was touched by the present of music that Elgar had brought him in the shape of gramophone records. Delius said that he had to depend upon the radio for his music in these days and he criticised to some extent the programmes that were broadcast. Elgar agreed – but then great musicians are *never satisfied that great music receives enough attention.'*

Another unattributed report said the two composers were: *'old friends. Distance has prevented close intercourse; but they have much in common besides the bond of nationality,'* while a further paper mentioned gifts which Elgar had taken with him for his stricken colleague including some records of Sibelius and Hugo Wolf, adding: *"Delius would not want to hear my music," he said in his modest way.'*

The Daily Telegraph printed Elgar's own account of the meeting which discussed Delius's love of Dickens. Elgar continued:

'Then the talk went round to older writers and I mentioned Montaigne, whose translation by Florio Delius does not know. He became at once tremendously interested. "Elgar has new ideas," he said to his wife and throwing up his left arm outstretched (his characteristic gesture when making a decision) "we'll read Montaigne," he declared.

'I inquired what prospects there were of seeing him in London. There is nothing Delius would like better and he is anxious to be present when his opera is performed. But the journey, the going from train to steamer and from steamer to train, is, for him, too arduous an undertaking.

'Having flown from Croydon to Paris, I suggested the pleasant alternative and pointed out how after motoring to Le Bourget he could reach London by aeroplane in less than two hours.

'The prospect attracted him. "What is flying like?" he asked.

"Well," I answered, " to put it poetically it is not unlike your life and my life. The rising from the ground was a little difficult; you cannot tell exactly how you are going to stand it. When once you have reached the heights it is very different. There is a delightful feeling of elation in sailing through gold and silver clouds. It is, Delius, rather like your music – a little intangible sometimes, but always very beautiful. I should have liked to stay there for ever. The descent is like our old age – peaceful, even serene.

'My description must have pleased Delius. Up went the left hand; "I will fly," he said determinedly.

'I told how the spell of being amongst the clouds was suddenly broken by the smell of whisky ordered by a passenger and carried past me – the horrible smell brought my mind to earth.

"Whisky!" said Delius, "the worst smell on earth ! But, Elgar, you have not become a teetotaller ?"

'With vivacity I denied the impeachment.

"Let us then drink a glass of wine together," said Delius. This seemed rather an astonishing proposition; but Mrs Delius, to whom I looked questioningly, interposed: "Oh, Frederick will join you."

'Champagne was brought and as we drank in the sunshine my old friend talked of present and past friends, of Granville Bantock ("the best of fellows," said Delius) and Percy Pitt, for whose musicianship Delius professed great admiration.

He concluded: *'The time passed all too quickly and the moment of parting arrived. We took an affectionate farewell of each other, Delius holding both my hands. I left him in the house surrounded by roses and I left him with a feeling of cheerfulness. To me he seemed like the poet who, seeing the sun again after his pilgrimage had found complete harmony between will and desire.*

'In passing through the pine-scented forest of Fontainebleau on the way to see Delius, I had come to a turn of the road leading to Barbizon. The scent recalled a scent of romance of 1880, and I nearly – very nearly – turned to Barbizon. After my visit to Grez I decided to go to Barbizon, but when I passed the crossroads the longing had passed away. That belonged to the romance of 1880, now dead. My mind was now full of another romance – the romance of Frederic Delius.'

These reports raise tantalising questions regarding the relationship between Elgar and Delius. Had they really met up in Leipzig as young men and enjoyed going to concerts together – and no doubt much else besides - all those years before ?

References to Elgar's meetings with Delius over the years remain scant – they may have encountered each other in 1909 when they both attended the Hereford Festival – though there is no reference in Elgar's wife's extensive diaries to any meeting, nor any reference that Delius may have visited Elgar at his Hereford home at that time. The two composers may also have been present at the 1912 Birmingham Festival - though again there is no evidence that they either met nor spent any extensive time together.

Yet Gaisberg's comments suggested that they were much closer friends than any hard evidence has supported – particularly his statement that they had spent what would seem to be some time together in Leipzig.

Available evidence places Elgar in Leipzig between December 31st 1882 and January 18th 1883. Delius is known to have attended the Leipzig Conservatoire between 1886 and 1888. There appears to be no evidence that Elgar travelled to Germany during that period, which would mean that they could only have met in Leipzig during the earlier time, when it is known that Delius, forced to work on behalf of his family's business, neglected his duties to visit the major musical centres in Germany. Whether this is the case is open to speculation as, again, there is no firm evidence.

However, there appears no doubt that Elgar and Delius enjoyed a friendship long before their meeting in 1933. A letter Elgar wrote to Sir Adrian Boult in advance of that meeting made reference to his excitement at the prospect of meeting *'my old friend Delius'* and from the nature of the records which Elgar took as a gift, he appears to have knowledge of the other composer's musical preferences.

His attitude towards Delius in this respect is somewhat unusual, as Elgar largely shunned relationships with his fellow composers. There was nothing of the friendship which existed between Vaughan Williams and Holst for example.

During his greatest years he had the opportunity on numerous occasions to have a meeting of minds with many leading composers – but apart from rubbing shoulders with them at festivals, there seems little evidence that he went out of his way to meet them – even such figures as Debussy, who lived for a while in England and who performed here. Indeed, perhaps the only mention of Debussy's name in Elgar's correspondence was a letter to his concert agents complaining bitterly that the French composer was paid more than him to conduct in London.

So this meeting was unusual to say the least, and furthermore, from the evidence of his comments about the visit, Elgar seemed strangely excited by Delius, and clearly revered him.

The Telegraph account, written by its music critic Ferruccio Bonavia, was to some extent carefully supervised by Elgar himself. A letter written to Bonavia shortly after the visit calls for a heading featuring portraits of himself and Delius, with a request that he wanted Delius depicted *'in the foreground'*.

He even suggested a headline for the article *'Elgar's Pilgrimage to Delius'*, and was particularly anxious that the reference to the *'scent of romance'* on the road to Barbizon should be included, as a note in Elgar's hand was sent to Bonavia containing the passage in full.

Such an attitude in old age contrasted with a rare reference to Delius when Elgar was in his prime. In an article in 1915 for the Westminster Gazette entitled 'Musical waterwheels – the devices that enable composers to 'carry on' by repetition' in which he criticised Debussy as well as Russian and British composers for using such devices, he added: *'possibly the most striking exception is Delius. My appreciation does not extend to all his works, but I cheerfully admit that he stands the water test astonishingly well...'*

The main problem with drawing any conclusion about this is that there is scant evidence of Elgar's early life. Apart from letters written by him at that time, there is no reliable chronicle of his activities.

However, it is a remarkable and tantalising possibility that Elgar, then in his early 20s and Delius in his late teens, could have met in the early 1880s, and formed a friendship which was to last throughout their lives.

This is made all the more remarkable, considering the somewhat questionable behaviour of Delius throughout his life.

Elgar and his entourage, particularly his wife, carefully cultivated the *'country squire'* image of Edwardian propriety.

It would be surprising, to say the least, to suggest that in his earlier life, that he had consorted with the likes of Delius.

It has been suggested that Gaisberg's reference to the two men being together in Leipzig was embellishment or even a fabrication, with a view to making the story more appealing to the press.

But why would he fabricate such a story when the story was strong enough anyway ? It seems too specific – not only suggesting they had met each other during that time, but gone to concerts together and played music to each other. The reference to Elgar's knowledge of Delius's taste in music also points to a suggestion that their relationship musically was hardly casual.

There is also the reference to the way in which Delius raised his left hand with the comment from Elgar: *'his characteristic gesture when making a decision',* as though this was something Elgar was familiar with.

Were this the first time that Elgar had ever met Delius, how would he know this ?

Furthermore these references were not contradicted by Elgar, despite his heavy involvement in how the article should be written and portrayed.

Without solid evidence one way or the other, this will remain yet another tantalising Elgarian *'enigma'* and it may be nothing but a fanciful notion that fifty or so years before their famous 1933 meeting, Elgar and Delius enjoyed a close friendship, involving concerts, their own fledgling music – and perhaps romantic encounters that in later life Elgar and his entourage made sure were deleted from his historical record.

However, there does remain one tantalising shadow of an evidence – in a letter written at the time to his friend Dr Charles Buck in which he described his activities in Leipzig:

'We used to attend the rehearsals at the Gewandhaus…the first thing I heard was Haydn Sym in G – the Surprise. Fancy ! I was astonished. I thought it strange to go so far to hear so little – After that I got pretty well dosed with Schumann (my ideal!) [Overture, scherzo and finale on 4 January, Symphony No 1 and songs on the 9th, Piano Concerto on the 11th] Brahms [Songs on the 9th, String Quintet op 88 on the 13th]. Rubinstein [Die Makkabaer, and 'Ocean' Symphony on the 11th] & Wagner [Parcifal Prelude on the 9th – only a few months after the opera's premiere. Lohengrin on the

12th. Tannhauser on the 14th], so had no cause to complain.'

And in a letter to his friend August Jaeger, written in 1899, he further recalled: *'I saw two dancers ...in Leipzig who came down the stage in antique dress dancing a gavotte: when they reached the footlights they suddenly turned around and appeared to be two very young & modern people & danced a gay & lively measure: they had come down the stage backwards & danced away with their (modern) faces towards us – when they reached the back of the sage they suddenly turned round & the old, decrepit couple danced gingerly to the old tune'*

This may, of course, be entirely unconnected with Delius – there is no mention of him, or even an oblique mention of someone who could be attributed to him.

However, Elgar's description of his activities, travelling around Leipzig and listening to music and playing himself, seems to ally very much with what Gaisberg mentioned in his press interview five decades later.

And to add one small further tantalising fact – which may or not be relevant – while in Leipzig, Elgar is known to have been in the company of a 17 year old student from the Academy and she wrote years later of the very activities they enjoyed together in Leipzig.

She wrote: *'...there was one or two important musical events which he was anxious to hear, amongst them*

Anton Rubinstein's opera which the composer was conducting...being a young female with time upon my hands, he asked me to get the tickets for the first performance. I took two or three places in a box...'

Her account seemed to mirror exactly the sort of activities which Gaisberg had mentioned, and it is quite possible that the young Delius, who would have been 18 at the time, might have been part of the group.

This is further enhanced by the identity of Elgar's young friend, whose name was Edith Groveham – and Edith came from Bradford, as did Delius.

Printed in Great Britain
by Amazon